# The Secrets of Scaled Agile

A problem solving guide

Timothy Field

# The Secrets of Scaled Agile

A problem solving guide

Timothy Field

This work is licensed under a Creative Commons Attribution-NonCommercial-NoDerivatives 4.0 International License

# Contents

1 - Describing the problem . . . . . . . . . . . . . . . . . . . 1

2 - Not fixing the root cause of problems . . . . . . . . . . 11

3 - Not practicing the Agile values and principles . . . . . 21

4 - Not believing in the Agile values and principles . . . . 32

5 - Not rewarded for agility . . . . . . . . . . . . . . . . . . 38

6 - Too much trust in the process . . . . . . . . . . . . . . 43

7 - Misunderstanding the customer's problem . . . . . . . 48

8 - Creating poor solutions . . . . . . . . . . . . . . . . . . 51

9 - Not understanding the type of shaping needed . . . . 55

10 - Unclear objectives . . . . . . . . . . . . . . . . . . . . 63

11 - Not structuring up front shaping . . . . . . . . . . . . 70

12 - No time for up front shaping . . . . . . . . . . . . . . 75

13 - Not clear on high level scope . . . . . . . . . . . . . . 78

14 - Not building in end-to-end slices . . . . . . . . . . . . 88

15 - Not using live data early when replacing a system . . 94

CONTENTS

16 - Poor quality low level requirements . . . . . . . . . .  98

17 - Poor preparation for big room planning . . . . . . . . 106

18 - Suboptimal organisational design . . . . . . . . . . . . 109

19 - Too much work in progress . . . . . . . . . . . . . . . . 116

20 - Lack of monitoring . . . . . . . . . . . . . . . . . . . . . 121

21 - Lack of project management skills . . . . . . . . . . . 133

22 - Suppliers competing . . . . . . . . . . . . . . . . . . . . 138

23 - Inexperienced leadership . . . . . . . . . . . . . . . . . 141

24 - Transformation without business involvement . . . . 145

Conclusion . . . . . . . . . . . . . . . . . . . . . . . . . . . . . 148

References and book copyright . . . . . . . . . . . . . . . . 149

# 1 - Describing the problem

Why should you read this book? If you are about to embark on scaling your agile software delivery or are struggling with it, it will help. Each chapter will identify common problems then show you how to tackle them. You can use this information to avoid them if starting out, or fix your situation if currently scaling. The advice here will help you improve however you are working, such as using a framework like SAFe, LeSS or Nexus. I have worked on very large scale projects and experienced these issues in real life. My perspective is a broad one including extensive consulting experience. I've also been in many different industries including finance, healthcare and marketing. These same problems come up again and again. Early in my career I didn't have enough knowledge to solve them and made big mistakes, more recently I've been able to help people avoid or fix these issues. I would have dearly loved to have had a book like this when starting out.

There are many great minds in the world, such as Malcom Gladwell and Dave Snowdon. This book intertwines their theoretical work, helping to explain the reasons we encounter problems alongside practical advice to help you improve. **These are the secrets to successful scaling.**

In case you are wondering, I haven't written this using any AI. I hope you find this book educational, thought provoking and ultimately impactful in how you work.

## Target audience

This book is written for people working in software development who ideally have a basic knowledge of Agile and Lean. I would expect everyone who works with software to get something useful from this book, from the person leading an organisation through to a software developer in a team. You may also be looking to improve your skills as an Agile coach or want to improve your product management capability. There are significant business benefits from following the guidance in this book, from faster delivery to improved outcomes. It is designed to be easy to understand, making the subjects it discusses as accessible as possible to everyone.

## Introducing the problem statement

Each chapter contains at least one problem statement that helps summarise where things can go wrong. These are written in a structured way using the following format:

- **The problem of** [description and root cause]
- **affects** [who]
- **the impact is** [what happens because of it]

For example:

- **The problem of** the trains regularly not running on time
- **affects** our employees
- **the impact is** 40% are late for work at least 2 days a week

There can however, be multiple people impacted:

- **The problem of** the trains regularly not running on time

# 1 - Describing the problem  3

- **affects** our employees
- **the impact is** 40% are late for work at least 2 days a week
- **affects** our organisation
- **the impact is** 10% of sales are lost due to meetings started late

In this example the quantified impact to the organisation is considerable! If you find you have one of the problems in this book, I would strongly recommend you quantify your own impact. This is particularly useful if you have several issues and need to know which to prioritise.

## Using the problem statements in the book

Use the problem statements in each chapter to identify and quantify the issues you have. The book can also be used with your team(s) in the following way:

1. Publish the list of potential problems in the book to your team(s) to see which apply.
2. Get them to write up the specific issues they have then identify and quantify them using the problem statement format.
3. After identifying a problem use the relevant chapter to gain more understanding of how to solve it.
4. Create actions to solve the problem and monitor the results.

The next chapter explains how to use problem statements in detail and includes a workshop for this process. Make sure you read this to get maximum value from the book.

## Reasons for scaling

The main reason we should consider scaling techniques is when we need to efficiently coordinate our delivery with multiple teams. If every team is able to deliver on its own it is better to let them do this. Small independent teams that are able to deliver valuable features in isolation should be the goal of every organisation. This allows us to provide value to market quickly and avoids the expensive overhead of multi-team planning and co-ordination. In many large organisations it isn't possible to achieve this, and we need to manage the way teams work together. This is often down to business or technical complexity. For example we may have a large number of software systems that need to be worked on to create a new business process. Where you have team co-ordination required, structured scaling methods should be more efficient and provide a faster time to market.

## Principles, frameworks and methodologies

If you want to learn about how to efficiently deliver software you will no doubt encounter the following terms:

- Principle: A fundamental truth that explains how something happens or works.
- Framework: A loose incomplete structure that can allow other practices to be included, but can still provide most of the processes required.
- Methodology: This is a prescriptive method with defined steps and rules.

Frameworks and methodologies are typically built upon principles. Both frameworks and methodologies require skill to implement. It is very easy to blame the process, instead of looking at your own maturity. When implementing these you should consider working with experts. Their experience will be invaluable.

## Weaknesses of methodologies

Imagine a world where, when you master it, one methodology could provide optimised product delivery consistently and successfully. You don't need any additional skills and the results are perfect each time. There are two key problems with this:

1. An organisation's needs can be very complex and these methodologies then need to grow and grow, adding layer upon layer of process in response to every possible scenario. As more criticisms are levelled, the methodology grows until it becomes huge and hard to implement.
2. The methodology is not complete enough to fit the scenarios it is used for, but despite these weaknesses no adaptation occurs.

## Weaknesses of frameworks

Frameworks suffer from different problems to methodologies, these are meant to be flexible and added to. They can suffer from these issues:

1. People don't add to them and treat them as complete. With these gaps the organisation doesn't function well.
2. People may not have the skills to add processes to the framework.
3. The framework grows in response to criticism and quietly moves more towards being a complex methodology. In this case you may see recommendations that it should not be adapted.

## The impact of principles

At their core frameworks and methodologies are based upon principles, such as this one from the Agile manifesto:

- The best architectures, requirements, and designs emerge from self-organising teams

Contrast this with the PRINCE2 principle:

- Defined roles and responsibilities

From the Agile principle we see a focus on self-organising teams, where people are encouraged to work together however they like, to achieve the best results. This means that if three developers wanted to get together to work out an optimised architecture this would be fine. This is very different to identifying a specific role for each task, such as an architect, and expecting that person to do the work. The downside of not defining roles and responsibilities is that no-one may take responsibility for certain tasks leading to a mess.

The Agile value of "*Responding to change over following a plan*" contrasts with many traditional plan based methods, such as waterfall, that look more like "*Following a plan over responding to change*". These often manage change via a formal change control process. This process can be complex and slow. In plan driven development it is often said that we fix scope then vary time and cost. However, in my experience we often see a focus on fixing all of these! Change will become the enemy in this scenario. Contrast this with Agile, which actively promotes change in order to improve customer outcomes.

# 1 - Describing the problem 7

🔓 Time   🔒 Cost   🔒 Time

**Agile**
Value Driven

**Traditional**
Plan Driven

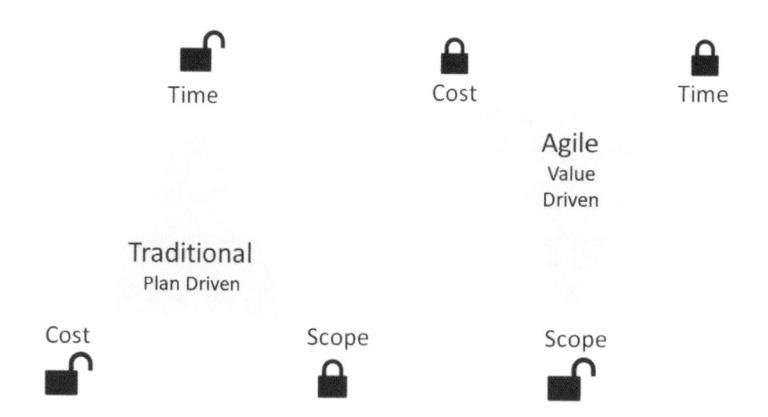

Cost 🔓   Scope 🔒   Scope 🔓

Does it matter if I'm using Agile methods but don't believe in the principles? Yes, at best it will cause conflict with those who do, and at worst it will remove the benefits of Agile. If my main priority is to fix scope, time, cost, and quality then I will resist change no matter what delivery method I am using. This is the where the phrase, *"doing Agile, not being Agile"* comes from. A common criticism of SAFe is exactly that, the idea that it is simply a waterfall-based system dressed up as Agile. This criticism is unfair and is true of any delivery method including Scrum when these are controlled by people who disagree with the core Agile principles.

## A brief history of scaling

As the news filtered through that Agile methods were working, and more and more organisations were becoming successful with them, they became more difficult to ignore. Existing popular methodologies and frameworks that had previously been taught as perfect were being challenged. Below is a description of a typical journey many organisations have gone through or are currently going through.

**Starting with Scrum**

Many organisations began embracing Scrum as the Agile framework of choice. Scrum is a lightweight team-based framework. *There is a great deal of information available about how this works and therefore it is not described here.*

Due to its lightweight nature, organisations began to find it difficult to implement into their existing structures. Scrum was not initially built for scaling; It was designed around small high performance cross functional teams. Serious questions arose around how a large organisation was supposed to cope with these new small teams consisting of a:

- Scrum Master - owns and controls the Scrum process
- Product Owner - owns the strategy and work backlog
- Development Team - the classification for anyone else

Companies were busy building multi-million-pound programmes in the way they always had, and were somewhat puzzled as to how things would now work. Serious questions around the new Agile practices arose:

- How do I fit my programme team, business teams, project managers and development manager into this?
- How do I get my products delivered if they're really big and I have lots of delivery teams?
- I guess I can follow the Scrum of Scrums for communication but is that all I need to scale this new thing?

Companies found themselves struggling with Scrum at scale and implementing its simple structure directly into a world of command-and-control project and programme managers. **The ways of working were changed but the belief systems weren't.** What usually happened was that a few developers and testers were allowed to play Scrum within their existing organisational structure. They were allowed to do what they want, as long as time, cost and quality were met. Change was met with resistance as soon as there was any sign of work running late followed by a return to low level planning and micromanagement.

Outside of the Scrum delivery teams sat traditional programme and product teams that specified and managed projects that were sent through the Scrum "sausage machine", to then be picked up by the service side of the organisation. This is known as Water-Scrum-Fall. Rather than seeing change as a positive, with rapid test and learn driving business benefits, project managers focussed on working out how to track progress. They started micromanaging teams using the number of story points delivered (a way of estimating) to predict when things would be done, whilst keeping a RAID log and reporting to a programme board. Although a little more uncertain than using the beloved Gantt chart it gave them some degree of control.

Companies tried to get more "Agile" by bringing in experienced coaches who were primarily tasked with improving estimation and delivering faster. They despaired at the existing set up, fixed as much as they could at the development team level and then departed to "rescue" the next place. Underpinning this was a conflicting belief system.

The Agile purists who were pushing for Scrum were defeated by the issue that different organisations and project sizes needed different solutions. As well as changing any process being difficult due to the people involved being unpredictable. If I run into a restaurant and shout, "Everyone get out!", the response may be completely different depending who is there. I can try and predict what will happen, but I don't truly know.

**New scaling techniques emerge**

As Scrum only implementations were causing big problems at scale, the industry responded with new frameworks and methodologies. LeSS (Large Scale Scrum), Nexus Framework and SAFe are examples of major players seeking to solve these issues. The industry is now fragmented with some very different approaches.

## Summary

So where does this leave us?

In this book I'm going to help you think differently, to aid your understanding of what the principles, frameworks and methodologies really mean to your organisation. I'm going to define problems and examples of these to help you understand how to improve. It is important to realise that you should not simply look for one "perfect" delivery method to solve all your problems. Let's consider (i) a simple defect that needs to be delivered and (ii) a multi-million pound financial system. We wouldn't put the same delivery structures around these two changes.

*For details on copyright and registered trademarks of the material used in this book please see the References chapter.*

# 2 - Not fixing the root cause of problems

Throughout the book, you will see problem statements and how to solve them. When working on your own problems it is possible to focus on fixing the symptoms and not the root cause. This results in changes that don't work or worse still do damage. This chapter contains many anti-patterns. An anti-pattern is a solution that superficially looks good but isn't. Look out for the anti-patterns below when seeking to understand and solve your problems. Use this foundational chapter to help you maximise the effectiveness of this book.

## Problem statement format

Problem Statements are one of the **most helpful tools** in understanding issues properly and aligning people. I cannot state strongly enough the power of these simple statements in fixing the right thing:

- **The problem of** [description and root cause]
- **affects** [who]
- **the impact is** [ideally quantified]

This chapter can now be summarised using the problem statement format.

- **The problem of** not fixing the root cause of problems

- **affects** organisations that are scaling
- **the impact is** fixes are applied that don't work or worse do damage

**We will now look at some common anti-patterns when writing problem statements to help you maximise your value of them.**

## Anti-pattern - No root cause analysis

The senior portfolio team determine that projects are being delivered very slowly. Each one seems to be taking too long, so the portfolio team tasks its project managers to get closer to the detail and micro manage all the work through. What failed here? With root cause analysis, it is determined that we are starting too many projects at the same time leading to teams switching between them and never finishing anything. After prioritising the projects for the teams and reducing the number in progress, the speed of delivery goes up. There are two possible anti-patterns here.

1. The senior portfolio team didn't do this on purpose, they **assumed** they knew the root cause. **This often happens when we've solved a similar problem before.** We feel we don't need to validate the fix before making it. This is summarised in the problem statement below:

- **The problem of** assuming we know the root cause as we have solved something similar before
- **affects** organisations that are scaling
- **the impact** is fixes are applied that don't work or worse do damage

2. The senior portfolio team **assumed** they knew better than their teams and didn't bother to ask them.

- **The problem of** assuming that because we are more senior we know more and can come up with better solutions
- **affects** organisations that are scaling
- **the impact is** fixes are applied that don't work or worse do damage

## Anti-pattern - Problem solving in silos

The following anti-pattern occurs when groups of people in specific roles, such as testers, get together to discuss problems and improvements. Let's say the test team identify a problem with the number of defects they are finding. They set up an improvements workshop but don't invite the business analysts and developers. They then assume that the development team are not doing sufficient testing of their own work because they are lazy. From this assumption they decide to monitor the number of defects per team and send a regular report to senior management. The idea is that by reporting on quality it will impact the developers poor attitude to testing. In reality the requirements being given the developers are not well formed and scenarios are being missed. The solution created won't work and will create conflict. This pattern is commonly seen when scaling Agile due to communities of practice for specific roles being set up. Before you do anything consider the knowledge and expertise of your team, do you need to involve more people?

- **The problem of** not involving the right people in understanding and fixing a problem
- **affects** organisations that are scaling
- **the impact is** ineffective fixes are applied that don't work or worse do damage

# Anti-pattern - Team strategy set in isolation

The marketing department see that they are losing customers to a competitor and formulate a new strategy. They decide to seek funding to step up their marketing campaigns. They focus on showing customers how great the new product features are. The results of the new strategy aren't as expected, despite the increased spending there has been two months of no change. The marketing leadership discuss the results with the department heads. A suggestion is made to run root cause analysis across the company to understand why we are losing customers. Each department is asked to contribute. After some analysis it is determined that the customers are not purchasing due to the website's speed being poor, in some cases the payment process takes up to 3 minutes to complete. The additional marketing is not solving the problem. It is driving a few more customers to the website, but the expected outcome is not being achieved. After the IT support team improve the speed of the servers customer sales increase. Cost and time to fix was a fraction of the new marketing campaign and was successful. It is very common for teams to create strategy in isolation, this can result in improving the symptoms of problems rather than solving them.

- **The problem of** creating team strategy in isolation and not understanding the root cause of poor performance
- **affects** organisations
- **the impact is** wasted effort on improvements that have low impact

## Anti-pattern - Difficult problems ignored

Sometimes we get difficult problems that will require major change to rectify. A part of the software system is unstable, often breaking when changes are made, frequently resulting in impact to customers. We know about this problem but it requires significant effort to fix it, so instead we put more testers on it and slow the delivery down. The team have raised this many times and have eventually given up discussing it. The problem moves into a state summed up by the phrase, "That's just how we work here". Organisations can have a lot of these problems and the accumulated impact of them all can be very high.

- **The problem of** some problems being very hard to fix and therefore being left broken
- **affects** organisations that are scaling
- **the impact is** slower delivery

## Anti-pattern - Teams not optimising the overall process

Another reason for ignoring problems is where the root cause is with another team. A software deployment team asks people to book time with them every time they need a deployment. Due to this booking system, there are major delays resulting in frustration. The deployment team manager doesn't want to change anything and is happy with their process. This process is set up to benefit the deployment team and their team over time has optimised it. After a while, the development team gives up asking for the situation to be improved.

- **The problem of** optimising locally without considering the impact to the wider organisation
- **affects** organisations that are scaling
- **the impact is** no fixes are applied and damage continues

## Anti-pattern - Lack of customer impact

Let's start with a typical problem statement:

- **The problem of** not explaining to our customers how great all our new features are
- **affects** our company
- **the impact is** a loss on average of 10 customers each month to competitors and $20k monthly revenue

At first view this problem statement may look good, it is well formatted and contains quantified impact. However, hidden in this is a problem statement built on an incorrect assumption, that customers are leaving due to feature information. The anti-pattern in this problem statement is that although it involves the customer the impact to them is missing. The "**affects** customers" and related **impact** statement are missing. This means we could be hiding assumptions. By understanding this danger we go and discuss with customers why they left us to get the real root cause. We can now define the actual problem:

- **The problem of** the web site availability being poor and crashing at least twice a day
- **affects** customers
- **the impact is** on average 30 important transactions lost per week that must be re-keyed, causing on average 8 hours of additional effort

- **affects** our company
- **the impact is** a loss on average of 10 customers each month to competitors and $20k monthly revenue

In addition to this, watch out for missing data. This is a big red flag as to whether research has been done to determine root cause. We now have a well-formed problem statement. This allows us to clearly see the impact to multiple parties, with the customer doing rework, and the organisation losing customers and revenue.

## Summary

As long as you avoid the anti-patterns in this chapter, you'll find problem statements are very powerful for increasing understanding and alignment. This is why I have used them throughout the book.

## Problem solving workshop

This workshop has been provided to help you add structure to solving your problems. Feel free to change it to fit your circumstances. When running this face-to-face I use post-it notes put up on a wall. For remote workshops I would typically use a tool like Miro.

**Workshop Purpose**
To identify big problems and tackle their root cause.

### 1. Problem statement training

Before you run any improvement workshops introduce the problem statement format. The following should take around 30 minutes with a group of less than 10. Ask people to draft a problem they face when travelling. As this will be a problem that they face themselves they should be able to quantify it. The quantification is very important as it helps you decide how big the problem is. The root cause is also shown in the example below:

- **The problem of** being late for work because of a slow puncture in my bike tires, meaning I must pump them up every few days
- **affects** me
- **the impact is** I am late 2 days out of 5 by 15 to 30 minutes

Next, review the problem statements the team have created. This may seem like a really easy exercise, but despite detailed instructions and examples I've had some people struggle with this. **If you can get people to read this chapter it will help a great deal too.**

## 2. Workshop preparation

- Decide on what you are going to focus on improving. You could be reviewing the list of problems contained in this book, or an area such as quality or working together.
- Identify the right group of people to attend the workshop, and if possible keep the attendees to around 10 or less.
- Ask people to do some research in advance and create a few high impact problem statements. These should contain the root cause of the problem. The quality of the work done up front will greatly improve the workshop outcomes so you may wish to review these up front.
- Make it clear that you only want problems that are large and are likely to happen again (avoid one off issues). Ask people to limit the number of problems they bring to around 3. They may need to prioritise.

## 3. Workshop

Consider blocking out 2 hours for your first workshop as it can be difficult to get good results if you are rushed. Run with less than 10 people until you are comfortable with the structure. All timelines are guidance only, you may change these to suit your own situation.

## 2 - Not fixing the root cause of problems

- Remind the team of the problem statement format. Also the importance of including the root cause and quantification.
- If the team have done the pre-work, put up any problems that people have brought with them. Ensure each problem has its own card. Get people to have a quick scan of these and group or remove any obvious duplicates.
- Allow around 5 minutes for additional brainstorming of problems people see. There is no rush here so take your time. It is fine to capture these as a simple description e.g. lack with unit testing, rather than writing a full problem statement. Quantify these where possible.
- Each person presents their two or three biggest problems to the group explaining the root cause, evidence and any metrics.
- If a problem has already been covered the person has the option to add to the existing problem i.e. they have more data, or delete theirs.
- As a group decide on the top two (or so) problems you are taking forward. Keep the number of problems selected to a minimum at this stage.
- Ensure those you select are good quality problem statements
  - Ask "why" this is happening to confirm the root cause.
  - Add quantification to the impact statement whenever possible.
  - Disregard any problems, no matter how big, that are very unlikely or certain not to happen again.
- Allow around 5 minutes to brainstorm solutions for a single problem.
- Select the simplest solution (size) with the highest chance of success (impact). You can map these on a grid if it helps. Ask the team to avoid putting up any low impact large size items.

**Size**

**Impact**

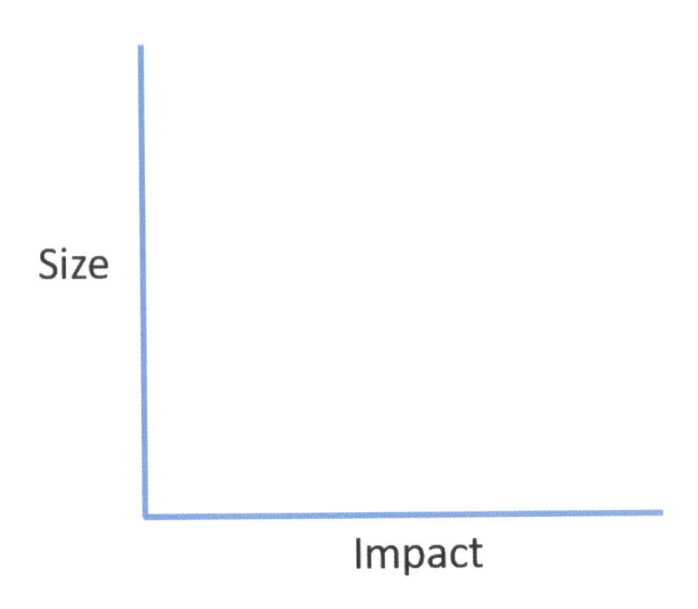

- Build out the solution. See the workshop output section below for what you need to produce. **You may need to stop at this point if you need another team to help shape or deliver the solution.** You can repeat the solution process for a number of problems if you have time.

4. *Workshop Output*

- An agreed problem statement.
- A clear solution with sufficient detail for everyone to understand it.
- A solution owner.
- A plan of action with tasks and task owners.
- A decision on how often you will meet to discuss progress.

# 3 - Not practicing the Agile values and principles

When scaling Agile we need to ensure we keep a focus on agility and not just a successful multi-team planning process. In other words, we should not lose the deliver fast, test-and-learn mentality that provides optimised results. This chapter shows how following the Agile values and principles affects success. A surefire way to fail is when people don't even know them. If I have just created a massive project with all of the features I can think of in a single large release, am I following this principle?

- *Deliver working software frequently, from a couple of weeks to a couple of months, with a preference to the shorter time scale.*

This can be summed up in this problem statement:

- **The problem of** not understanding the values and principles behind Agile leads to poor outcomes due to the lack of feedback and adaptation
- **affects** customers
- **the impact is** an increased risk of a poor experience and lower levels of satisfaction
- **affects** organisations that are scaling
- **the impact is** worse business results

# Values and principles

Most frameworks and methodologies have their own list of principles. Many delivery methods claim to be "Agile" (LeSS, SAFe, Scrum etc.), each having different principles for achieving success. There are certainly overlaps between their principles, but they are not always the same. It can be difficult to understand **why** they work in a particular way if you only focus on their processes. Although the PRINCE2® methodology (copywrite AXELOS Ltd) is not often described as "Agile", it is introduced here to show the impact of its principles and the mindset that sits behind it. I will use this to demonstrate how a delivery method that is not aligned with Agile can cause problems when rapid testing and learning is required.

**So why include lists of principles?** Aren't they just long, boring and unimportant, and haven't we all seen them before? I often find that people who have been working in an Agile environment for years are unfamiliar with them. Even some Agile coaches have struggled! Being aware of these principles can have a major effect on how we work. **Consider each of the values and principles and what they mean in your situation.**

## The Agile Manifesto - values and principles

The creation of the Agile Manifesto was a groundbreaking moment in the software industry. It involved 17 industry experts meeting up to define what is now one of the most important outputs of all time. This is the foundation for what most people call "Agile".

The four Agile values:

- Individuals and interactions over processes and tools.
- Working software over comprehensive documentation.
- Customer collaboration over contract negotiation.

## 3 - Not practicing the Agile values and principles

- Responding to change over following a plan.

*That is, while there is value in the items on the right, we value the items on the left more.*

A common misuse of these values would be to view the items on the right as having no value, you then end up with no firm processes, no documentation, no planning and therefore no commitment to deliver to a timescale (a controversial subject I'll not discuss here).

The primary benefit of Agile is acknowledging that we do not know everything up front, and we need to learn as we go. Our solutions emerge as we work on them. This is summarised in the value *responding to change over following a plan*. There is also a strong emphasis on people working closely together, with face-to-face communication being preferred to processes and tools. In the first principle below we have the customer in primary place too, with delivering to them early and often being given the highest priority.

The twelve Agile principles are:

- Our highest priority is to satisfy the customer through early and continuous delivery of valuable software.
- Welcome changing requirements, even late in development. Agile processes harness change for the customer's competitive advantage.
- Deliver working software frequently, from a couple of weeks to a couple of months, with a preference to the shorter time scale.
- Business people and developers must work together daily throughout the project.
- Build projects around motivated individuals. Give them the environment and support they need, and trust them to get the job done.

- The most efficient and effective method of conveying information to and within a development team is face-to-face conversation.
- Working software is the primary measure of progress.
- Agile processes promote sustainable development. The sponsors, developers, and users should be able to maintain a constant pace indefinitely.
- Continuous attention to technical excellence and good design enhances agility.
- Simplicity–the art of maximising the amount of work not done–is essential.
- The best architectures, requirements, and designs emerge from self-organising teams.
- At regular intervals, the team reflects on how to become more effective, then tunes and adjusts its behaviour accordingly.

## The PRINCE2® principles (copyright AXELOS Ltd)

Let's compare this with the principles that sit behind the PRINCE2® methodology. It is worth noting that PRINCE2® is not a software specific methodology. It was originally developed for the UK government. It is primarily used in highly regulated environments and for managing predictable work. In other words, it was not designed for work that needed a lot of test and learn. PRINCE2 Agile ® came later and was in response to this need. This new methodology is aligned with the Agile values and principles.

In PRINCE2® the business justification is key. This is usually in the form of a business case that may contain several different business options. These can be evaluated before choosing the one deemed most effective to plan against. The project team refers to the business case throughout their delivery, this is to ensure that any proposed changes to the scope align with the expected outcomes. There is also an emphasis on carefully managing each project

# 3 - Not practicing the Agile values and principles

stage to completion. Please note this is a simplified description of PRINCE2®, for full information see the official AXELOS website. These are the principles:

- Continued business justification: The project is based on a sound business case.
- Learn from experience: Review what you've learned so you can improve.
- Defined roles and responsibilities: A strict project structure making is clear who is responsible for what.
- Manage by stages: Regular review points with the Project Board after each stage. Decisions made as to whether to continue.
- Manage by exception: Tolerance limits so management knows when to step in. These are time, cost, quality, scope, risk and benefits.
- Focus on products: Planning, controls and quality are all product based.
- Tailor to suit the project environment: The project's environment can change based on factors such as size, risk and complexity. Management can therefore split or combine roles, processes and documents.

## The cost of not including Agile principles

Most principles that underpin the various delivery frameworks make sense and are hard to argue with. However, what people miss is a more subtle problem:

- **The problem of** delivering non-predictive work using a framework or methodology that resists or makes change difficult

- **affects** customers
- **the impact is** an increased risk of a poor customer experience and lower levels of satisfaction
- **affects** organisations
- **the impact is** worse business results

### Non-predictive work and PRINCE2®

PRINCE2® is more suited to predictive work, because it seeks to manage time, cost, and quality. A project manager is responsible for a project plan and projects are delivered in stages. As the project progresses any changes required to it are carefully managed. The management of change can be in the form of a formal change control board, where each suggested change is assessed for value. One of the principles that appears to welcome change is *Learn from experience*, but this is about documenting what you learned from the project and applying it to the next project. Now it is possible you learned that customers didn't like your last feature and to test it earlier, but this is a stretch and is not as clear as this Agile principle: *Welcome changing requirements, even late in development. Agile processes harness change for the customer's competitive advantage.* This Agile principle actively encourages change and any methodology or framework built upon it must do too.

### An example PRINCE2® issue

A business case document is created by a senior product leader to justify a new customer focussed mobile application. This is reviewed by the senior team who point out gaps and help firm it up. This includes detailed financial modelling that predicts success. During the annual planning event a prioritisation exercise is undertaken. This business case is selected, further confirming its value. Finally, the new mobile application idea is discussed with the whole company generating a good deal of excitement. A plan is created to deliver the application with a 7 month timeframe.

## 3 - Not practicing the Agile values and principles

The problem occurs, that although the business case contains a lot of detail, it also contains a number of important assumptions about what the customer wants. As the business case has had so much internal validation, its success becomes a guarantee in the leadership's minds. These high risk customer desirability assumptions aren't questioned. The application is finally released and customers don't like it, a year later it is scrapped at considerable cost to the organisation.

It is not surprising that this could happen. Without the Agile values and principles we will be tempted to treat the outcome of our work as a certainty. Even though the project may have been perfectly managed in terms of time, cost and quality it has failed to achieve the expected outcomes.

By ignoring the big assumptions hidden in our business case we are not following these Agile principles:

- **Changing requirements** - *Welcome changing requirements, even late in development. Agile processes harness change for the customer's competitive advantage.* With Agile we don't see work as an analysis task allowing us to fix our scope, followed by the creation of a detailed plan to deliver it. We see the work as evolving and changing based on regular feedback.
- **Continual improvement** *Our highest priority is to satisfy the customer through early and continuous delivery of valuable software.* With Agile we don't see work as a single project with a fixed scope to be completed, but as a product that should be released early and continually optimised. **This is very important for innovation work.** It is a mistake to think you can release a new product to market and expect to get it right first time.

I have my own real-life example of this problem. A £20m project was undertaken to put product offerings online. Customers could select a plan and buy it without any human interaction. Previously the sales team would discuss and personalise plans for customers. This change had a business case and significant benefits expected from it. A great deal of excitement was generated, as this was going to be a big win. There was little to no customer testing. On release, customers bought less plans! The company was facing a downturn in sales. Although the plans were easier to buy, the customers did not fully understand them. They were priced higher than the competition and customers used the new website as a basic comparison tool. This was a very costly failure.

## The cost of ignoring Agile principles

Now we will consider what happens if you take an agile delivery method and misuse it.

- **The problem of** using a delivery method and ignoring the Agile principles contained in it
- **affects** customers
- **the impact is** an increased risk of a poor experience and lower levels of satisfaction
- **affects** organisations that are scaling
- **the impact is** worse business results

**Scrum (Agile)**

A common methodology that follows the Agile values and principles is Scrum. I will now give a simplified explanation of Scrum, as there is a huge amount of information available on this online. Small self-sufficient teams (usually less than 10 people) seek to complete a batch of items from a prioritised product backlog every iteration (usually lasting two or three weeks). There is a business representative called the Product Owner who works within the team to create, refine and prioritise the work item backlog. Each work item should be complete and in a fit state to be potentially shipped each iteration. This leads to the creation of a Minimal Viable Product (MVP). Scrum can be scaled with a Scrum of Scrums where members of different Scrum teams, such as developers or Scrum Masters, talk with each other regularly to coordinate change and manage dependencies. We will look at whether this is sufficient later in the book.

**An example Scrum issue:**

A large new software feature is given to a team to build. This work is broken down into small pieces that are completed every 2 weeks. After 6 months the feature is ready for release to customers. The customers receive the feature and hate it. The usability is terrible and it is missing important pieces of functionality they need. This results in a similar outcome to the PRINCE2® example earlier in the chapter, but for a different reason. We are not following the Agile principles, even though the Scrum methodology is built upon them. Feedback from customers is not being gathered regularly.

# Agile frameworks do not guarantee agility

In most cases, you will hear from the owners of scaled frameworks that theirs are "Agile", and from detractors that they are not. Some delivery methods naturally align themselves with learning, containing processes that make it easier to achieve. This certainly helps, but in most cases, it is the implementation that determines success. Water-Scrum-Fall where Scrum is misused is perhaps the most famous Agile anti-pattern, although some people in the IT industry seem to think it is a good thing! It is defined as doing up-front analysis and design stages, then building a large fixed scope in many small iterations (usually every 2 weeks). After it is built it may go through a verification stage, before being released to customers.

## Summary

Regularly review the Agile values and principles to see how well you are following them. If you are using an industry standard Agile methodology or framework such as SAFe or LeSS, you should review how well you have implemented it. Selecting one of these does not guarantee you are working well. Companies with custom delivery methods should pay particular attention to their Agile processes.

- Are you aware of the Agile values and principles?
- Do you have test and learn activities undertaken before you release your work to customers?
- Is responding to change easy for everyone, even if it impacts timelines?

## Agile principles and delivery framework workshop

### Purpose

To drive positive change by evaluating your scaled Agile delivery method against the Agile values and principles.

### Process

For this workshop you should have an expert running it who can help guide conversations. Depending on how long you have, you may wish to cover just one value or principle. Avoid rushing as the conversations can be challenging. Run this process for each one:

- Explain the selected Agile value or principle (or a principle from your own delivery method) that you wish to discuss. You may wish to prepare up front for this. For example with

this one: **Agile value** - *Individuals and interactions over processes and tools*. I would explain that relying too much on processes and tooling can lead to a lot of documentation and inefficient slow hand-overs. I would ask people to think about how much discussion is taking place and overall how effective they are at working together.
- Each person to score how well this is working (1=many issues 5=fully optimised)
- Make a note of why you scored it this way
- You can now have the following discussion:
    - How is your delivery method supposed to be working?
    - What changes will you make to improve the current situation?
- Record actions and owners

**Output**

- Actions with owners and clear success criteria. Your delivery process owner may take actions to improve your framework or methodology.
- Consider follow-up meetings if the actions are large enough

# 4 - Not believing in the Agile values and principles

This chapter shows how people's beliefs in underpinning principles affects success. We will cover two problems in this chapter starting with this one:

- **The problem of** not agreeing with the Agile values and principles
- **affects** customers
- **the impact is** an increased risk of a poor customer experience and lower levels of satisfaction
- **affects** organisations that are scaling
- **the impact is** worse business results

How are you going to cement change in your organisation and ensure you succeed? A surefire way to find your good intentions undone is where people's beliefs conflict with the changes you want to make. It can take a long time to unlearn the entrenched beliefs that drive peoples' behaviour. The most useful way to use principles is to see if they conflict with your actions. For example, if I have just created a massive project with all of the features I can think of within a single large release, am I following this Agile principle?

*Deliver working software frequently, from a couple of weeks to a couple of months, with a preference to the shorter time scale.*

# The impact of belief

Over time as we take actions based on our beliefs, these achieve results and reinforce or disrupt them.

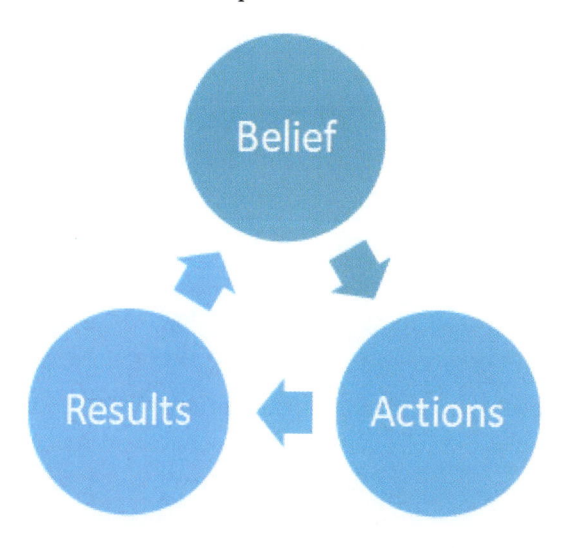

One of the most effective ways of altering an existing belief system is to try something new yourself and see it work, rather than just to be told what is right.

Consider a project manager who for years has delivered projects on time and perfected the planning and micro-management of delivery. They pride themselves on hitting deadlines. They have beliefs firmly held up by results. What they did worked and the results re-enforced this belief.

Old beliefs can gradually be overridden as people build up enough results. However, the opposite is also true, large scaled agile implementations that fail can cause lasting organisational damage. The belief that Agile principles work is destroyed and a plan based command and control delivery system is put back in. This is why it is so important to get your scaling methods right. The concept of "fail fast" is often described as an acceptable strategy in Agile communities. The idea is to learn quickly from failure. However, this can cause big problems as failing does not reinforce your belief system. It is best to avoid failure where you can as it can have a high hidden cost.

When starting to scale Agile by introducing a new framework or methodology:

- Do this at a scale where you can avoid failure

Avoid changing your entire organisation all at once, especially when putting a new delivery method in place. You should take time to embed this into an area and get it working well; This gives you a strong case study and many advocates for the new ways of working.

- Give time and space for change

Do not immediately demand faster delivery and punish people for missing delivery deadlines. If you are working with an external consultancy make sure you give them the time and space to upskill and embed the changes too. If you don't provide the time it will cause teams to avoid the cost of test and learn. The new methods will become a burden and be quickly dropped. Senior managers should introduce the change clearly in this way, and avoid punishing people at all costs.

- Support with experts

It is one thing to put a new method in place, it is another for people to master it. A good example I find is Objectives and Key Results (OKRs). As the name suggests this is a technique for summarising your strategic Objective and measuring it using a few Key Results. It is very easy to understand at face value, however, the teams I have worked with have needed upwards of a year to be able to achieve success. Do not underestimate how much effort it is to change a way of working. You will need to regularly course correct. Ensure you have enough expertise to help people through the journey.

## The prioritisation of principles

It is often not as simple as to say that people don't agree with the Agile values and principles. On face value they are easy to agree with. What matters is **where their priority is**. This gives us our next problem:

- **The problem of** not prioritising the Agile values and principles
- **affects** customers
- **the impact is** a poor customer experience and lower levels of satisfaction
- **affects** organisations that are scaling
- **the impact is** worse business results

Let's take the four Agile values:

- Individuals and interactions over processes and tools.
- Working software over comprehensive documentation.
- Customer collaboration over contract negotiation.
- Responding to change over following a plan.

What if we flipped the prioritisation of these such as *Following a plan over responding to change*? We now have a big problem. You ask a project manager who has always valued planning to do this and it will cause internal conflict, at worst they will simply not adhere to this value. Their previous aim of hitting deadlines is now replaced with methods that embrace change. This creates a situation where a lack of control is felt. The reason we embrace change is to improve our outcomes, but this was never what the project manager's performance was judged on. We need the project manager and the rest of the organisation to believe that project outcomes are the priority and not delivery deadlines. It is beneficial to achieve both, however within reason, the priority shifts to outcomes. If the impact of these new values and principles aren't properly considered you will meet fierce resistance often in the form of criticising the new ways of working. Make exposing their priorities a priority.

## Summary

Having people who don't believe in the Agile principles or don't prioritise them can be a big reason why you fail to achieve agility in an organisation, regardless of the delivery method you are using.

When successfully implementing new ways of working you will see beliefs changing. If you are failing, look to course correct quickly or existing beliefs will solidify and cause long term damage.

## Agile beliefs workshop

**Purpose**
To drive positive change by challenging people's beliefs in the Agile values and principles

**Process**
For this workshop you should have an expert present who can help guide conversations. Do not rush people, especially if discussing organisational issues. You may also wish to invite senior people who have the power to make changes.

- Take the Agile values and principles, or any other specific principles that you wish to discuss. E.g. **Agile value** - Individ-

uals and interactions over processes and tools. You may wish to prioritise a few values and principles to have an in-depth discussion or run a longer session (i.e. 1 day) if you want to cover all of them
- For each value or principle discuss
    - What does it mean to you?
    - Do you agree with it? Each person to score (1=no 5=completely)
    - Discuss the scores where people don't agree with it
    - What personal changes will you make to move closer to this value or principle?
    - What organisational changes are needed to move closer to this value or principle?
    - Record actions and owners
- Schedule follow up meetings to track actions

## Output

- Actions recorded with owners and clear success criteria
- Consider follow up meetings if the actions are large enough

# 5 - Not rewarded for agility

There is more to people's motivation than their own beliefs. They are also motivated by what they are rewarded for. This leads us to the next problem:

- **The problem of** rewards not being linked to the values and principles of Agile
- **affects** customers
- **the impact** is a poor customer experience and lower levels of satisfaction
- **affects** organisations that are scaling
- **the impact is** worse business results

*"You get what you reward"* as written in Michael LeBoeuf's book (1985) *"The greatest management principle in the world"*.

In the last chapter, we covered what happens when we don't believe in the Agile values and principles. In particular, we looked at the Agile value of *Responding to change over following a plan*. Taking this a step further, if we reward our project managers for the opposite, hitting end dates and punishing them for not doing so, we will firm up their priorities. This organisational behaviour will not embed agility. The typical response to this is that Agile fixes time and cost but varies scope. The truth is as soon as scope change occurs (such as important customer feedback) we will see it as a risk to timeline, rather than something positive. This ends up forcing processes like taking decisions to change control boards. In reality, this is simply making change difficult. These processes are seen as a positive by the organisation as they represent control but are very harmful to the ability to quickly inspect and adapt.

The situation when implementing agile delivery methods is made even worse when you have roles like user researchers who are specifically rewarded for getting feedback to drive positive change. They will despair of the additional process controls and a fight will ensue. Both are being rewarded for conflicting principles. The organisation needs to be honest with itself. The argument for control is that spending is kept under tight limits ensuring Return on Investment (ROI) is maximised. The problem with this is you will see no returns if customers do not like or want your product!

## Organisational culture

Quinn & Rohrbaugh in their Competing Values Framework (1983) describe company culture. For this chapter, we will simplify the description of this model to focus on its impact on Agility. You will see the four quadrants below.

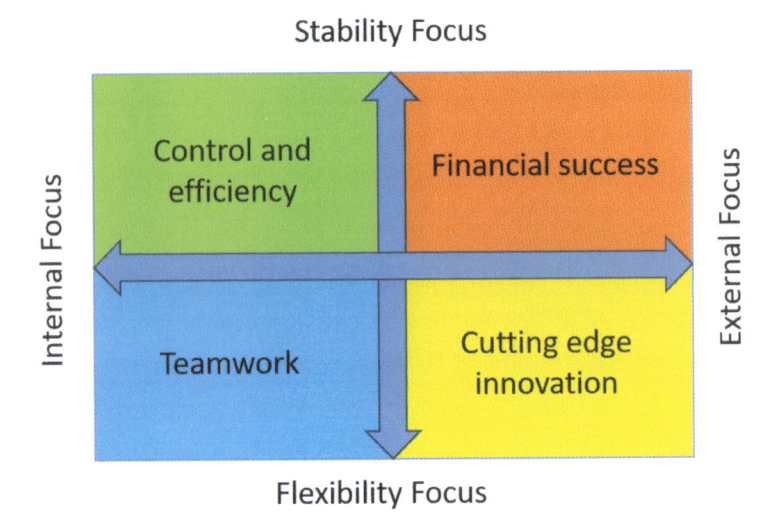

```
                    Stability Focus
                          ↑
    ┌─────────────────────┼─────────────────────┐
    │                     │                     │
    │   Control and       │  Financial success  │
    │   efficiency        │                     │
Internal                   │                    External
 Focus ←───────────────────┼──────────────────→  Focus
    │                     │                     │
    │   Teamwork          │  Cutting edge       │
    │                     │  innovation         │
    │                     │                     │
    └─────────────────────┼─────────────────────┘
                          ↓
                   Flexibility Focus
```

The majority of organisations will say that they are people focussed (teamwork in the grid), prioritise financial success, have good delivery controls in place, and deliver some cutting edge innovation. In other words, they paint a picture of being optimised across all of these quadrants. The truth is unlikely to be this simple. It can be useful to consider these as priorities rather than absolutes. When dealing with assessing organisational agility we are most interested in the impact of a culture of control and efficiency. **The organisational culture will determine how people act and are rewarded.**

## The impact of a control culture

In heavily regulated environments such as payment systems in banks, where innovation work may not be very common, a control and efficiency culture may be necessary. You should ensure that you are familiar with the organisation's situation before advocating for Agile and innovation. When developing systems like those that handle payments, there is little margin for error, and we are likely to be using detailed analysis to avoid mistakes. We cannot afford to put out broken software!

In situations where agile delivery methods are appropriate:

- An agile culture that values innovation will promote the need to test and learn, which means following the principle *"Responding to change over following a plan"*. With this type of work, we can use timeboxed iterations, but detailed planning will be seen as unhelpful and wasteful.
- A control culture will still try its best to create a plan, and then closely track time, cost and quality. By building a detailed plan we will be ignoring our risks, such as if the customers really want the product we are building.

You can gain a better insight into organisational culture by:

1. Looking at their delivery methods to see how test and learn is implemented (if at all)
2. Asking about past work to determine their real behaviour. We want to know when agility was required, did the organisational culture limit or stop it. Use these questions to gain insight:

*Using examples of how you have managed innovation work:*

- What up front customer or technology risks did you identify?
- How and when did you de-risk these? (note: there should ideally be some activity before the software is released to customers)
- What outcomes did you achieve versus what you expected?
- Could you have improved these outcomes by doing some earlier testing?

**If an organisation's culture of control is to be challenged, it is essential to demonstrate that their behaviour is adversely affecting their outcomes.**

## Considerations at scale

The pressure to exert control increases as the investment and timescale increase. When we scale, we also bring with it more planning and coordination effort. This additional overhead means that changing direction becomes more difficult and ultimately costly. This can lead an organisation to focus on control.

To counter this:

- Move to **smaller work items** that can be delivered faster
- Do lightweight up front testing before the full build to validate any assumptions, such as showing a customer a sketch of a screen

## Summary

Optimising an organisation's culture is an important lever to improving outcomes. By keeping the size of deliveries down and our scaling planning to a minimum, we enable our teams to change direction for much less cost. In turn, this increases the chance of the organisation accepting Agile practices. Attitudes and ultimately the culture will begin to change when optimised outcomes become the primary success measure. You should reward people for seeking to improve outcomes above that of hitting timelines and praise the early testing work that reduced risk. The people responsible for timelines must be aware that it is OK to take longer if the outcome will be improved. When you assess people's performance begin by asking about the results the team achieved and how they used agile practices.

# 6 - Too much trust in the process

One of the main issues with process problems is that we get too wedded to how we are currently working. This is where we are convinced our delivery methods are perfect and we just need to get better at them.

- **The problem of** not fixing or replacing a suboptimal delivery method because we believe it is not the method at fault, but our ability to implement it
- **affects** organisations that are scaling
- **the impact is** late delivery, poor outcomes and poor morale

## Single and double loop thinking

This is a useful technique for challenging our own mental models. It was created by Chris Argyris who wrote an article entitled Teaching Smart People How to Learn (Harvard Business Review, May/June 1991), Harvard Business School. Let's use an example to demonstrate it. Try to answer this question and see how you do.

You are a consultant who has been put in charge of the queueing experience at a bank. Customers are bored waiting especially at the times of the day when the bank gets very busy. What solutions can you think of that will help?...

Perhaps you came up with some ideas like this

- Add interesting posters for people to look at

- Increase the number of queue lanes
- Change the layout of the bank

These types of ideas are representative of single loop thinking. The correct answer is to look at the root cause of the queue and not give any solutions at this stage. Maybe you discover that the online banking website is hard to use, and is driving people into the bank. As soon as this is known you should fix that and not even try to fix the queue. The queue is simply a symptom of an underlying problem. This is double loop thinking.

In double loop thinking we seek the solve the root cause of the problem, which could be the underlying process. This requires a shift in our mental model and is especially hard if we implemented a process that isn't working well. This is hard because at the time it was created we **believed** it would work.

## Too busy to fix the process

When work starts to run very late it becomes really hard to think differently, as you get too busy firefighting to fix things. We can then switch to single loop thinking by default. The temptation here is to focus on reducing scope, implementing much stricter change control and increasing planning. Although a focus on these things can be beneficial it does not always fix the underlying root cause.

I worked on a project where the delivery had major problems and was running late:

1) There was only a loose way of tracking the completion of high level scope to understand what was left.
2) The teams responsible for delivery had not paid attention to shipping on time and had spent too long tweaking and changing things for low value. One team re-did a single process 3 times over many months. As the team had spent so long tweaking the project

it could no longer be delivered in time, even when high level scope was understood.

What was needed was a wholesale shift in how people were working, getting a handle on high level scope, being able to track the overall progress, and avoiding low value change. Instead of this single loop thinking fixes were applied, and more tracking was added. The additional micromanagement just created more admin, which slowed things down further.

# Triple loop thinking

This further expands on the single and double loop model. Here we add another factor, which is the impact of people's beliefs and the company culture. If we take the previous project as an example you would seek to understand people's motivations so that you can challenge them. **We do this by being clear on what we are trying to achieve**, such as delivering a project on time. We can then challenge people by showing how their current knowledge and ways of thinking have not resulted in the expected outcomes. In other words, we need to challenge people on the principles they believe in.

Consider the Scrum Masters in my previous example where the project was running very late. They believed that all change is beneficial and saw scope management as wasteful. Let's examine how triple loop thinking can be implemented in this scenario. We start by being clear on what we are trying to achieve, which is delivering the work in a timely manner. It is not acceptable to build for as long as we want, as a) this delays value to the customer and b) costs a great deal of money. We can demonstrate how their way of thinking has not provided the expected results, as scope and timescales are out of control. We are now challenging core beliefs and assumptions. This can be very hard for people as it creates something called "cognitive dissonance". This is where beliefs conflict with new information. In this scenario, you will need to have patience, and in some cases give people plenty of time and space to think through the "new reality". When people can move beyond their existing beliefs, you can open the door to exploring new and innovative solutions.

## Impact at scale

There is a big problem with some scaled agile methods. If they are marketed as perfect and you believe that, you will not practice double and triple loop thinking and challenge their processes. This creates a mindset of *"I am at fault"*, when things don't work well. A truly dangerous mindset to have. The question you should ask here is whether or not the delivery method is being improved over time by its authors. If so, it can be inferred from this that even the authors do not think that it is perfect.

## Single loop response - just work harder!

As our work starts to run late a common single loop thinking response is to get the teams to work more. This can yield positive results. However, teams are only able to run at a high speed for a limited amount of time before getting tired and slowing down. The Health and Safety Executive (HSE)* have worked to produce guidance around fatigue and its impact. Their first Key principle in fatigue is: *Fatigue needs to be managed, like any other hazard.*

In jobs where there is a risk of physical accidents fatigue has been shown to be a major factor. Therefore, it becomes obvious that this needs to be managed, but it is not so clear when working in software environments.

*Reference *HSE Guidance - Human factors: Fatigue*

Related to this is the agile principle:

- Agile processes promote sustainable development. The sponsors, developers, and users should be able to maintain a constant pace indefinitely.

## Single loop response - reduce quality!

Another solution that appears effective is to shift quality right, in other words, focus less on up front requirements, less on design and see our throughput go up. This looks good initially, as more is developed but is simply loading very expensive risk onto either end to end testing, or worse still to the customer.

## Summary

It can be very easy to slip into single loop thinking especially when timescales are short. Step back and consider the root cause of your problems. The problems may be caused by people's deeply held beliefs. If this is the case, be clear on what you are trying to achieve before you challenge them. Finally, if the delivery method does not address the problems you have then consider changing it.

# 7 - Misunderstanding the customer's problem

In the next two chapters we take a closer look at creating a test and learn culture to meet our customer's needs and why it is so important. In simple terms, this is based on two questions:

| What problem does the customer have? | → | What are we going to build to solve this? |

## Not understanding the problem's root cause

In this chapter we will focus on the first question, where understanding a problem can go wrong:

> What problem does the customer have?

Our product owner has specified the following problems for the team to solve:

- Customers aren't buying on our system because they can't do one-click credit card payments.
- Customers love our products but are put off by the décor in the shops.

- Our customers aren't happy with our current paper process because they hate filling in forms.

These problem statements all sound sensible and therein lies the problem! After we have spent months building features we see our sales stagnate. We covered a lack of root cause analysis when looking to fix a scaled process previously (chapter 3) and the same issue is applied here.

- Customers aren't buying on our system because they can't do one-click credit card payments. *Real problem / root cause:* Cost of postage is very high and when they come to pay they drop out.
- Customers love our products but are put off by the décor in the shop. *Real problem / root cause:* Two large security guards at the front door are putting people off entering.
- Our customers aren't happy with our current paper process because they hate filling in the form. *Real problem / root cause:* We don't warn them to bring ID then when they get here they have to do two trips.

This leads us to this problem statement:

- **The problem of** people believing that they understand the root cause of a customer problem but don't, leads to the wrong solution being built
- **affects** customers
- **the impact is** a confused unhappy customer
- **affects** organisations
- **the impact is** lower profit and potential loss of market share

# Solving a small problem

However, there is another layer of complexity here! It is often not as simple as the person defining the problem not knowing anything. They may have **some** evidence but not enough.

- **The problem of** people believing that they are solving a large customer problem by relying on anecdotal evidence when it is, in fact, a small problem
- **affects** customers
- **the impact is** a small number of them are happier
- **affects** organisations
- **the impact is** lower profit and potential loss of market share

The quality of your evidence can be a serious issue and one that is more difficult to detect. Let's take this one as an example where we said that we got the root cause wrong:

- Customers aren't buying on our system because they can't do one-click credit card payments.

Perhaps they just had a major complaint from a customer where they said this. These pieces of information can impact the mind of the leader, moving their view away from the definition of anecdotal evidence, but in reality, it is still in this category. **We end up spending a lot of money creating a solution for a problem that is not very big.**

Using quantified problem statements is the best way to avoid this. If the leader had written down how many people the problem affected they would have had to admit it was from one customer!

## Summary

The two issues of solving the wrong problem and not solving a big enough problem are amplified at scale. The reason for this is we are potentially running large multi-team expensive releases. Use quantified problem statements to help you avoid this situation.

# 8 - Creating poor solutions

In the last chapter we looked at what happens if we get the customer problem wrong or if the problem isn't big enough. Now we will focus on the second question and consider what happens if we get the solution wrong.

| What problem does the customer have? | → | What are we going to build to solve this? |

## Defining the problem

Consider a senior leader creating a business case with projected earnings in it. These documents can be very high quality and take considerable time and effort. In reality, many of these are guess work, and should be viewed as such.

There is a real danger of building solutions that are nothing more than someone's idea of useful without even realising that these need testing. This usually plays out when a senior leader first gives a solution idea to a team. The leader confidently explains the purpose of what is being built and the benefits that are expected. This situation is compounded when the idea sounds good to everyone. Nobody bothers to ask what the customer thinks of the solution and building starts.

- **The problem of** people believing their solution does not need validation or improvement

- **affects** customers
- **the impact is** they are given features they don't want or can't use
- **affects** organisations
- **the impact is** lower profit and potential loss of market share

## Using prototypes for feedback

Prototyping is a very useful technique for validating ideas. Visual prototypes can be much easier for people to understand than descriptions. Imagine describing a house to someone and how long it would take, what if you showed them a sketch? This does not discount the need for written specifications but augments them.

Good examples of prototyping can be found in the User Experience Design (UXD) and the software development disciplines. On the UXD side, there are many visual prototyping techniques such as high fidelity interactive, paper, wireframes etc. All of these are useful when clarifying a solution. On the software development side, you can create working prototypes by running a timeboxed "spike" to de-risk specific areas. Consider prototyping when you can quickly deliver something to remove big risks.

## Other feedback techniques

User Experience Research, also known as UXR, is another discipline that specialises in gathering feedback from customers. Within UXR there are many feedback gathering techniques such as customer surveys, ethnography (going and seeing what people do in practice), one to one interviews, group discussions etc.

# Up front feedback cost

One of the main reasons for arguing about gathering feedback up front is the time it takes. This should be proportional to

1. the risk involved in what is being built
2. the time it would take to put the feature live
3. the cost of getting it wrong

A major root cause of conflict here is when building is often seen as more valuable than customer testing. **In particular an idle development team is seen as the worst offence.** The pressure to "get on with it", can become very big. They may agree with customer testing if the build team are busy.

- **The problem of** people believing solution validation is less valuable than people being busy building
- **affects** customers
- **the impact is** they are given features they don't want or can't use
- **affects** organisations
- **the impact is** lower profit and potential loss of market share

To avoid this you should consider two key measures

1. *"How many of your ideas didn't achieve the benefits you were expecting?"*.
2. *"What is the customer satisfaction rating of the feature / product you built?"*.

## Summary

Focussing on measuring the benefits achieved and customer satisfaction metrics is the best place to start. This builds a business reason for user testing and prototyping. Without this you are likely to be having conversations based on opinions and beliefs.

# 9 - Not understanding the type of shaping needed

One of the frequent misunderstandings of Agile methods is when and how to apply them. Let's say I'm working on a VAT calculator that has a set of business rules to follow, should I apply the same way of working as someone who's building new screens for a customer? This can be summarised in our problem below:

- **The problem of** not understanding when it is most appropriate to apply Agile methods
- **affects** organisations that are scaling
- **the impact is** confusion with the value of Agile and how to implement it successfully

## Introducing the Cynefin Framework

The Cynefin ® Framework was invented by Dave Snowden in 1999 and its initial application focussed on how a manager should act (or make sense of) situations with different levels of complexity. It has since been broadened beyond management.

This sense making technique, helps you analyse your situation using domains. Each domain helps you to work out the most appropriate way to act. This model can be extended to help us understand the different types of work we will encounter and how we should deal with them. In the Cynefin Framework below you can see 4 main domains. We'll now look at each in turn and see how they can help us.

**Cynefin Framework**

***Cynefin Framework as at February 2021 by Dave Snowden – thecynefin.co***

The Cynefin® Framework as of February 2021—reproduced under Creative Commons Attribution 4.0 International licence from Cynefin.io (2021).

## Applied to our work

How I am using the framework is not universally agreed upon, but I find it helpful, and those I have taught have as well.

**Clear**

Here in the clear domain, we have a simple task like updating a colour scheme on each screen. The problem is easily understood and can be optimised, leading us to a "Best Practice" single solution. We can create repeatable processes here. Project planning using a Gantt chart with tasks and resources will be a good solution to managing a backlog of work. As the work is clear, we wouldn't need much analysis to solve the problem.

Here's how to use the full framework

- **sense** - Gather details about the problem
- **categorise** - Identify it as a known type of problem
- **respond** - Follow the best practice solution

*How to manage this work - Consider a basic Gantt chart with the typical delivery time allocated to each piece of work. You should not need to break these pieces of work down into a lot of detailed tasks.*

**Complicated**

I'll start with an example to help explain what this domain means. Let's say I'm building a VAT rate calculator. I have created calculators before and know the options I have that will work. I could perhaps create a separate program for the calculator or add it to an existing one. I may have different ways of deploying it, to its own server, or as part of an existing one. As an expert, I can do analysis to figure out the solution. The fact that there can be more than one solution means we will choose the one that's most appropriate. In the model, this is defined as "Good practice".

If I do a lot of work in this domain the introduction of Agile ways of working with its focus on emergent design, rapid feedback and user testing may seem nonsensical to me. In fact, when working in domains where people are doing repeatable complicated analysis Agile methods may add unnecessary overhead. An example of this was an Agile transformation I ran in a bank, it had a mainframe team who were writing complicated scheduling jobs. The idea of breaking these down into smaller deliverables, like user stories, and incrementally delivering and testing parts of them wasn't helpful.

Here's how to use the full framework

- **sense** - Gather details about the problem
- **analyse** - Analyse the problem and work out the best solution
- **respond** - Build the best solution

*How to manage this work - Gantt charts with detailed tasks work well in this domain. Make sure you set aside enough time for analysis. Incremental delivery, which means delivering something in stages, is a good option if it is possible. We can also run this in a scaled environment where each team's work is planned out in detail.*

**Complex**

In this domain, we can't use analysis alone to give us the right solution. We are in the realm of very tricky problems that can't easily be analysed, such as those requiring customer opinion. In this domain, we are firmly in the best area for Agile methods. This strongly relates to the Agile value, "Responding to change over following a plan". We should be using feedback to achieve better outcomes by building, learning, and changing as we go.

One of the main reasons analysis fails here is that people don't know what they want until they see it. The biggest mistake that was being made over and over again was to deliver products with an uncertain outcome (complex) as if it had a certain one (complicated). Now it isn't that you don't receive the feedback, it is just the high cost of getting it late. Imagine a customer waiting a long time for version 1 of a completed product and them not liking it, or worse still, not being able to use it.

This can still happen when people are using "Agile" delivery methods. This is where we actually practice analysis based techniques under the guise of Agile. For example, we could be doing analysis and creating a big backlog of user stories up front, then building them in 2 week iterations, and finally, after several months we go live. This is when the customer sees the work for the first time. There is no test and learn here, we are not practicing Agile at all, even though we may be using some popular Agile artefacts.

So how do I know if I'm in this domain? We can use the assumptions mapping technique. If you aren't familiar with this, you'll find an explanation in the chapter *Not structuring up front shaping*. If we identify desirability assumptions this provides a strong indicator that we're in this domain. Anything that requires a customer's opinion means we cannot use analysis to determine the best result. We need to test with the customer, ideally early. Testing our feasibility risks should also be considered, especially if they would take a long time to solve them using analysis. One common test and learn technique is building a technical prototype in a timeboxed spike.

*How to manage this work - This is where you should use Agile delivery methods. Use techniques like assumptions mapping to understand where your main risks to success are.*

Here's how to use the full framework

- **probe** - Run experiments to better understand the problem and suitable solutions
- **sense** - Gather key findings
- **respond** - Adjust the solution based on key findings

# Chaotic

In this domain, we need to fix something quickly and don't have time for a long test and learn cycle. Something could be badly wrong and we need to apply multiple fixes fast to hopefully find the right one. This isn't very common when building features, and would more likely be in situations like when a live server is crashing, or when we have a hacker who's got into the system. We may then act by deploying multiple fixes simultaneously to see which works. "Novel practice" is found here, where new or interesting solutions arise.

Here's how to use the full framework

- **act** - Do something quickly to see if it fixes a problem
- **sense** - Gather key findings
- **respond** - Adjust the solution based on key findings

## From Complex to Complicated?

Agile is often described as **value driven** where scope is variable with cost and time fixed. In traditional delivery methods, the focus is on being **plan driven**, where scope is fixed and time and cost vary. In reality, plan driven and value driven often end up with a desire to fix all three, but Agile in its true form would vary scope simply because it does not seek to do all the analysis up front.

# 9 - Not understanding the type of shaping needed

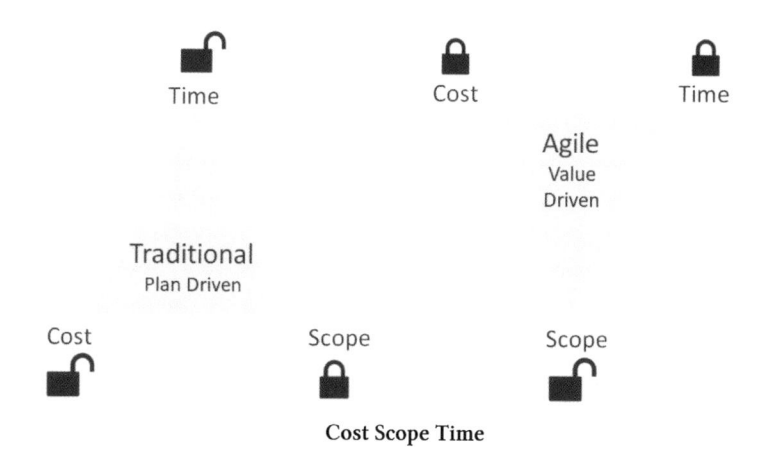

|  | Traditional<br>Plan Driven | Agile<br>Value Driven |
| --- | --- | --- |
| Time 🔓 | Cost 🔒 | Time 🔒 |
| Cost 🔓 | Scope 🔒 | Scope 🔓 |

**Cost Scope Time**

In Agile we seek to fix cost and time, which means we must have some level of certainty in order to do this. This is why identifying and removing the big assumptions up front is so important. Leaving these big risks to be tested after we have fixed our timescales will add a significant likelihood of blow out. Working through these risks up front allows us to move towards being able to fix time, and even though we should still be practicing test and learn, it is not as radical as questioning the whole solution. With these big assumptions removed, we are still unlikely to move back into the complicated domain and therefore go back to relying solely on analysis.

## Cynefin Framework and scaled Agile

As we can be running a really complex set up when scaling you should always consider how much up front analysis you do. Even if you are in the complicated domain doing all the analysis up front can be very expensive. This is just the sheer effort of getting everything right in one go. In this case break the work down into smaller parts, then incrementally analyse and deliver it. If you have many teams contributing to an end-to-end process look to get this integrated early. The analysis required to get large scale systems working end-to-end can be very time consuming. Therefore, delivering end-to-end functionality with a test and learn approach is highly recommended and will significantly reduce timescale risk.

## Summary

The Cynefin Framework is a powerful tool for understanding the situation you are in, enabling you to act appropriately. I find this very valuable for aligning teams on why Agile matters and when it is best to use it.

## Personal thanks

Special thanks to Jules Yim from The Cynefin Company for reviewing this chapter!

# 10 - Unclear objectives

If you want to understand how clear your strategy is, ask your teams this simple question, *"What is the company's strategy?"* (if you're in a large organisation then replace company with department). I have asked this question to many teams, at best this usually ends up being a list of features, and there's usually a long quiet pause! An even harder question would be *"What results is the strategy expecting to achieve?"*

- **The problem of** not being clear on why we're doing something and the expected results
- **affects** organisations that are scaling
- **the impact is** not being clear when the work is done and poor outcomes

## But we have a strategy!

This often ends up being a long-winded description with the background and solution described at a high level. These long descriptions look good, however there can be big problems with them.

## Objectives and Key Results

OKRs have become much more common in agile circles and are now seen as good way of being clear on the strategy. For those of you that are familiar with these this section may seem like one you can skip, but please don't. I have seen many anti-patterns with this technique despite it looking relatively simple. This chapter will cover these to ensure your strategy is clear. **OKRs are deceptively difficult to get right** and having coached these extensively I still see people a year after first being taught struggling with them. This chapter will not include how to scale OKRs through an organisation.

## The OKR format

**Objective**: a summary description of why you are doing something starting with a verb (increase, decrease etc.)

- **Key Result 1**: From x (baseline metric) to y (target metric) by date (stretch / committed)

Let's start with an example:

**Objective**: Decrease the number of complaints from customers

- **KR1**: From 400 complaints a month on average to 300 by June 2025 (stretch)
- **KR2**: From 3 people handling complaints full time to 2 by June 2025 (stretch)

The benefits of the **Objective** statement

- We have to summarise why the strategy is being done in a simple statement. This is much clearer than long descriptions, which can be hard to understand.
- Long descriptions can also hide a lack of alignment as to the true reason why something is being done. They can contain multiple reasons for change, making them even more unclear.
- As the objective is so clear it allows us to focus on what matters.

The benefits of the **Key Results**

- Being able to measure the impact of any change is very important and the key results do this for you in a very clear way. Not only do they measure the expected result they also contain the baseline you are starting from. When the baseline is missing this will indicate that more research should be done to understand the current state.
- Being able to define what results we expect indicates how radical the change needs to be. If we try and double our results, we can no longer tweak existing solutions, we have to think outside the box.
- Having metrics allows us to track our progress.
- As results come back, if we find they are not what we wanted we can pivot our strategy or even stop the work entirely. We may also stop the work early if we meet our goals. This is a great reason to build incrementally rather than ship everything in one go. You can adjust your strategy faster.
- A frequently missed but powerful aspect of KRs is the ability to stretch or commit to them. This is very important. If you ask a team to commit to a target that is outside of their control i.e. customer satisfaction, they will aim low. This makes it clear if the change is predictable (committed) such as achieving a security accreditation by a certain date. A mismatch in expectations can occur when stretch isn't labelled by a team aiming high. When they don't hit the results they are treated as failures by the management team.
- The timeboxed nature of KRs allows us to think about the size of investment we are willing to make.
- Timeboxing can also reduce the time to market. By looking for results regularly, such as quarterly, the expectation of faster delivery is set.

## OKR anti-patterns

In this section, I will cover typical problems I see with OKRs. It is possible to do these very badly.

### Objective anti-pattern - describing the solution

Rather than thinking about why we are doing something we describe the solution in the objective.

- Incorrect - Implement the new SQL database
- Correct - Decrease the cost of database storage

Writing the solution in the objective like the incorrect example above is worse than you think. The people building this may not be clear that it is about cost and could create a more expensive solution. They may have an assumption that they are doing it because the new database will be faster.

It is possible to provide strategic guidance with a broad change area, but be careful you don't include a specific solution, for example:

- Correct - Increase the number of bank customers in Egypt
- Incorrect - Increase the number of bank customers in Egypt by running 4 new adverts on television, in the next 3 months

### Objective anti-pattern - going too broad

As per the previous example, we could just say *Increase the number of bank customers* but this doesn't give any guidance to the team. It does not contain a strategy, it is just a desirable metric to move. Adding Egypt to the objective would perhaps tell us that they could do this in different countries and Egypt is the priority. You could perhaps add more direction but it is clearly a strategy and not a solution. These are typically your highest level OKRs, guiding departments or longer-term initiatives. Just remember the broad direction should describe the strategy, not a specific solution.

## KR anti-pattern - measuring the solution

This is the biggest problem I see, let's use an example to demonstrate it.

- **Objective** Increase the readability of documents
- **KR1** From 90 documents that are poorly formatted to 75 rewritten by June 2024 (committed)

It is much easier to measure the number of documents rewritten but this isn't the actual outcome. We want a metric that tells us if the objective has worked as we could re-write these very badly. Let's improve this OKR:

- **KR1** From 90 documents with a customer satisfaction rating of below 30% to 70% by June 2024 (stretch)

Here we are checking the customer satisfaction rating, giving us the real outcome. One of the main reasons people don't measure the outcome is it can be much harder. It is harder to get the baseline metrics and check the results. Although I do see people doing this anti-pattern over and over again by accident.

## KR anti-pattern - data too hard to gather

Some data takes a lot of effort to get, for example having to do customer interviews every time you need feedback can be expensive and slow. Where possible choose a metric that can be automated and is easy to gather.

If you have a metric but can't get the base data immediately you may wish to take a risk and set up the data collection method as part of the work. This is a good tactic when you are doing smaller pieces of work, it would however represent high risk if implementing a major strategic investment.

## KR anti-pattern - vanity metrics

To understand these, it is important to differentiate between leading and lagging indicators. Let's take a runner who's doing a marathon in 6 months. The result of this marathon is a lagging indicator. It is called lagging because it will take so long to get the result. The runner wants to see if they are making progress before the marathon. This is where leading indicators come in. The runner tracks their 10K time each week to see if it is improving. The 10K time is useful but ultimately it doesn't matter if it is improving if the result of the race is bad.

A vanity metric would be where we don't measure the race result but focus on 10K times getting better. Let's look at a real example from a company seeking funding to show how these can be misused.

The company rents out rooms to clients online. It wants to show good results to get people to invest. The company shows a graph of the number of people signing up as interested and another of the number of rooms being registered for hire. These are leading indicators. However! the company only provides this information to seek investment. What is not shown is the lagging indicator of the number of rooms booked.

Within our KRs we should always have lagging indicators and can have additional leading indicators where it makes sense.

# The cost at scale

The cost of getting your objectives and their respective measures wrong can be very high when working with many teams. You can end up with a lot of different requirements being added as mandatory due to a mismatch of understanding. This can initially be identified when senior leads are focused on preparing high level work items, then running prioritisation sessions. At their heart, prioritisation techniques usually compare value and cost. The results of the sessions may look good but the fatal flaw is that value is not defined. With value being subjective leaders can justify why their scope should be added. It also allows for scope creep later on, where new functionality cannot be adequately challenged.

MoSCoW is a common prioritisation technique that has this problem.

- The M stands for Must Have.
- The S stands for Should Have.
- The C stands for Could Have.
- The W stands for Won't Have.

In MoSCoW sessions you will see a very high number of work items added to M and S categories, and rarely any discussion of how they contribute to metrics. This results in a large amount of scope bloat.

## Summary

At scale, the risk of your goals not being clear can be very costly. Use OKRs to define and measure your strategy, it is a really powerful technique for:

1. Gaining alignment on your strategy
2. Measuring what matters
3. Ensuring initial scope is valuable
4. Stopping scope creep
5. Tracking progress allowing a pivot, or stopping early if results aren't as expected
6. Stretch your KR targets for greatness

# 11 - Not structuring up front shaping

In the chapter *Creating poor solutions* we covered the second question below, asking what should we build and covering why testing this up front is important.

| What problem does the customer have? | → | What are we going to build to solve this? |

The theory here is sound, however what may not be clear is how to put this into practice. This leads to questions like, "How much time should I spend testing and what should I test?". The following problem summarises the situation:

- **The problem of** not being clear how much up front testing needs doing
- **affects** organisations
- **the impact is** not enough validation leading to poor quality outcomes or too much leading to delayed releases

## Assumptions mapping

Assumptions mapping is a technique that you can use to help identify risks to success and decide how to remove them. Some of the riskiest assumptions can cause total failure and you may wish to solve these up front. You classify your assumptions against the following categories:

- Desirability - Do customers want this?
- Feasibility - Can we build this?
- Viability - Will the company achieve its goals (does the business case work)?

The most important of these is desirability. You should not spend time looking at different solutions, and spending time doing detailed financial modelling if the customer does not want what you are offering.

We begin by listing out any assumptions we have made within the three categories. It can be useful to start these with, "I believe that...". For example, a viability assumption could be, *"I believe that storing the data in SQL Server will be cost effective."* Avoid listing assumptions that don't carry much risk, we can filter these out without writing them down.

### Assumptions mapping grid

The assumptions mapping grid then allows you to prioritise your assumptions.

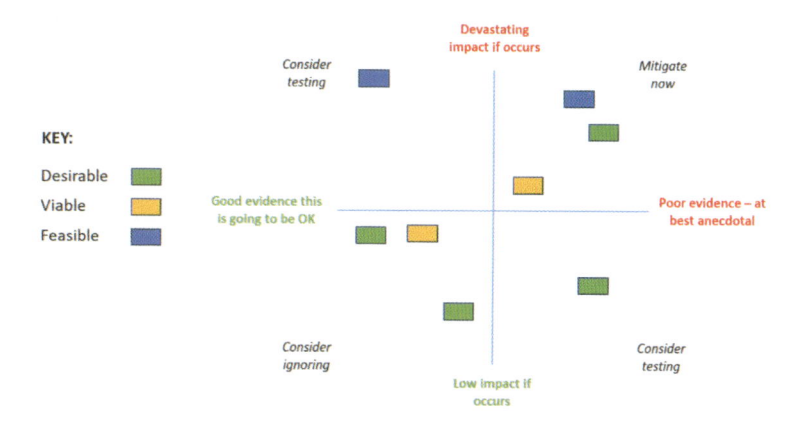

The y-axis gives you the impact. Devastating impact means your product will fail. If the impact is low you may choose not to test this at all. The x-axis then considers how much you know about this assumption, at its worst, you have no evidence that it is going to be OK.

Let's run an example grid mapping exercise against the last viability SQL example, *"I believe that storing the data in SQL Server will be cost effective."*

I will now work out where it sits on the grid:

- **Y-axis** We start by working out the impact of this going wrong. In this case, if we are wrong about the costs, it could wreck our business model. We know customers don't want to pay much more for our new solution. This places us towards the top of the Y-axis (devastating impact if occurs).
- **X-axis** Next we need to map the evidence level by seeing how much we know about this. I have previously worked on SQL Server costs and have some idea about them. I have good enough evidence to know roughly it's going to be cost effective at the scale we're at. Therefore, it sits towards the left (good evidence this is going to be OK). We these two factors discussed we can place the assumption in the upper left quadrant. I then decide it's really easy to test as I can quickly look at the SQL prices on the internet. So in this case, I'm going to mitigate it immediately and may not even record it.

**The power of assumptions mapping**

The ability to identify and prioritise key risks in the form of assumptions allows us to define our risk appetite. This helps justify how much testing we want to do up front in a structured way.

Let's run another example to show the power of this. Let's say the senior leader has said, "Customers aren't buying on our system because they can't do one click credit card payments," to justify their new feature. In our previous chapter, we showed how not quantifying the problem statement would mean this could slip through and get built. Now we apply assumptions mapping that will again catch this before build. We start with desirability assumptions and discover the leader has only anecdotal evidence that this is a problem. We decided it's easy to test this with our drop out rate data and customer feedback forms. 2% of people are dropping because of this. This assumption is removed relatively easily and the whole feature is stopped. The senior leader is happy that they have not wasted time on this.

## Up front testing at scale

Now relating this to scaling. In many cases the cost of a new feature or product is very high, we have a lot of teams involved and it can be a big commitment. So what if we'd spent a year building a large and complex product without considering customer desirability or if it made commercial sense? I think you can guess the outcome! This could result in a hugely expensive failure. Assumptions mapping can be run against the overall business case of these large initiatives as well as at a smaller feature level to identify and remove the risks up front.

## Taking assumptions into live

It should be noted that we can't always remove all our assumptions up front. Things like product market fit are typically discovered after a product goes live. These would be our viability assumptions. In this case record the assumptions and test them post release. For example, you may have a set a price and can't easily test if this will work up front. After a few weeks you see how well your product is selling and adjust accordingly.

## Summary

Use assumptions mapping to understand how much risk you have and run low cost experiments to remove it. Even if you can't remove this up front you will be aware of it and well placed to react when results come in.

# 12 - No time for up front shaping

Organisations have a strong desire to avoid people being idle and in particular, keep developers busy working. This can lead to pressure for our up front test and learn activities to be as short as possible. This leads to the following problem:

- **The problem of** not giving enough time to explore customer problems and solutions before building
- **affects** customers
- **the impact** is a poor experience and low satisfaction
- **affects** organisations
- **the impact is** lower profit and potential loss of market share

## Dual track Agile

A very useful technique for ensuring that there is time for research and exploration is dual track Agile. When scaling using timeboxes, such as 8 week build periods, we have time for shaping activities. It is important to avoid too much interruption to the development teams as multi-tasking is inefficient, but they should still be involved. The final output of this activity is a sufficient backlog of items that can be fed to the teams for the next timebox.

| Shaping Item 1 | Shaping Item 2 | |
|---|---|---|
| | Building Item 1 | Building Item 2 |

Timeline

To make this work in a scaled environment you may have a shaping team working in advance to validate problems and ideas. It is important that the team shaping the solution also contain technical people as they can help ensure the solution is feasible. If you are going to have people involved in both shaping and building cycles then ensure they are senior enough to manage their workload. Being aware of the cost of multi-tasking is important too, so avoid quickly switching between building and shaping. Perhaps doing half a day or more on a task and ideally completing it.

## Dual track Agile anti-patterns

### Timeboxes too short to shape

The typical Scrum set up of 2 week sprints can cause issues here where if you are really shipping features to customers this regularly it gives you very little time to shape. This leads to a focus on preparing requirements for the development team and not testing with customers. The argument against this would be, *"We'll find out when it is live"*. Yes, this is a good point, however there is a hidden problem here. If you are putting new features live on this regular basis you may be changing things that customers don't want, or adding functionality that has no value. In many organisations the removal of features is rarely done. The problem with these features is that the cost is not just in building and testing them. You also have to maintain them, support them, explain them and even market them. The combined effort here can be very large and if a team is continually putting out poor features it will have a significant detrimental effect on customer satisfaction. To fix this you may want to run a longer shaping cycle alongside a number of 2 week sprints. Make sure you are checking your results with customers too. Finding out after 6 months that all your work led to lower customer satisfaction would be a very poor result.

### UX team perfecting outputs without feasibility analysis

A big anti-pattern is a UX team running ahead with design and frustratingly being told *"No we can't do that"*, by developers after all their work is done. The typical response from a design team is that they don't want to be limited by technology or the solutions will never be optimal. This is true and it's good to have a clean break with technology constraints. The subtle thing here is that the ideas should be low fidelity prototypes and not fully polished screens. Then technology feedback can be given and ideas further shaped without a high level of wasted effort.

**Shaping always fills the timebox**

Another anti-pattern here is that each shaping activity lasts the same amount of time as the scaled iteration (e.g. 8 weeks). These should be seen as a backlog of shaping activities. Some should **stop early** if a user need is proven to be an incorrect assumption or a solution won't work. Run one shaping at a time to avoid people multi-tasking too. If every single feature you shape ends up being built this is a warning sign that you may not be making shaping decisions properly.

## Summary

Dual track Agile is a very effective method for giving teams time to test and learn. This gives the space and time for the job to be done well, leading to optimised results.

# 13 - Not clear on high level scope

The chapter that covers ensuring our overall objectives are clear will act as the foundation for solving the next problem. If your overall objectives aren't well defined then start there.

- **The problem of** overall scope not being clear and therefore not managed
- **affects** organisations that are scaling
- **the impact is** work that doesn't seem to ever be finished and significant lateness

## Defining requirements

The waterfall method handling scope was to create very detailed documents starting with analysis, then moving on to design. The idea here was that we could capture everything required and sign off. The problem with this was the complexity of creating these documents meant a very long up front cycle. The other issue is that they could be so complex you wouldn't be able to determine what was wrong with them until they were actually built. Big up front analysis would make sense if we were building a bridge where it is too difficult to change and the cost of failure is extremely high. In software we are rarely in this situation but if we are you should still consider up front analysis, see the chapter on "Not understanding the type of shaping needed" for more details.

## Out of control

When delivering product features most Agile methods would recommend breaking them down into smaller items that can be built and tested (even if not released), rather than building a whole feature in one big block then testing it. Agile teams are used to focussing on these smaller work items as units of progress. In Scrum you would typically see many of these work items delivered every two weeks. This works well when building small features.

At scale it gets more complex. We can have many features that need building involving many teams. If we are not clear on what these features are and how complete they are we can hit major problems. When each team only focuses and reports on the delivery of small work items it is hard to see the damage of adding more to our overall timescale.

More and more items added over time

As work is added incrementally it could look like we are on target to complete on time, but in reality, we are hiding huge amounts of work. The work tracking in this scenario may suggest that we are 1 month away from completion and everyone is happy, however this is hiding the fact that scope is completely out of control as more and more is added.

This is what may really be happening and it is even worse than first thought. Below we see 3 large features.

## 13 - Not clear on high level scope

**Work item 1**

More and more items added over time

**Work item 2**

**Work item 3**

High level work items not started yet

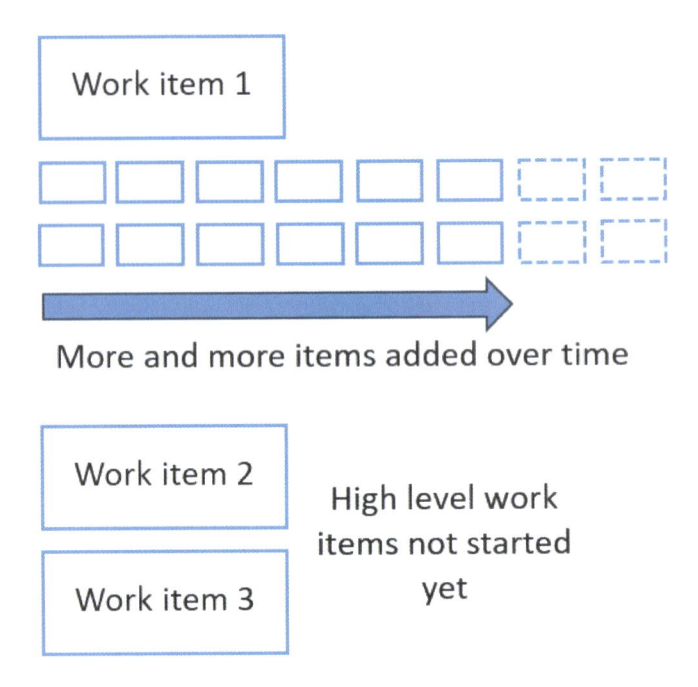

Huge amounts of time are being spent on the first feature. Items 2 and 3 are not even started.

The really large issue here is where teams are disconnected from the people tracking progress and do not have an eye on timelines. As this can have such a high impact, I have added the following problem statement.

- **The problem of** teams not prioritising an end date, not controlling scope and continuing to add work to the backlog
- **Affects** organisations that are scaling
- **The impact is** work that doesn't finish and unmanageable timelines

The could be several root causes:

- Cultural - where they don't see delivering on time as a priority and view all change as beneficial and valuable.

- Accountability - where they don't feel accountable for delivering on time, i.e. it's someone else's responsibility to worry about it.
- Big picture - where they are unable to see the big picture and cannot therefore deduce that their part in it is running late.

## High level scope definition

We need to overcome this problem and it starts by simply defining what your high level scope is. This may seem obvious, but a good question to ask any scaled agile leadership team is, *"Show me a list of work items that represent your high level scope"*. If they cannot agree on this list, you are already out of control before even looking at what the teams are doing.

## MVP & MMF definitions

Minimum Viable Product (MVP) or Minimum Marketable Feature-set (MMF) are two terms often used for defining what feature richness a new product needs before it can be fully released. When both are used together, MVP is usually used to describe the sufficient scope to learn about the product and MMF to describe what a fully complete chargeable product looks like. For simplicity I will stick with MMF for now.

The scope of this should achieve the following:

- Have sufficient functionality to at least fulfil the basic needs of the customer
- Be of sufficient quality for user to be satisfied with it (both bug free and usable)
- Have enough feature richness to be marketable against competitors
- Be competitively priced in the market

- Should meet the expected goals of the customer (i.e. solve a big enough problem for them)
- Should meet the goals of the organisation (i.e. impact organisational Key Performance Indicators / OKRs)

From this definition we can define our high level scope / features. The trick here is to REALLY focus on what matters and not to add any additional work.

Additional work has the following costs:

- Slower to market
- Low value features must be supported and maintained. Therefore, it is not just the cost of delivery that should be considered
- There are opportunity costs when delaying your product release including competitors catching you and lost revenue

## MBI definition

Another concept that is useful is Minimum Business Increment (MBI). This is used where you have an existing product and are adding functionality to it. The idea is to create the minimum increment of business value that will achieve your goals. Like the MMF this focusses the team on getting value to market early. Your MBI could still be large if it is to be marketed as a new chargeable software feature, and like the MMF it also asks the question, "How much do we really need to deliver to get value to ourselves and the customer?".

## Breaking down requirements

In order to overcome the problems of very detailed analysis and design documents we should only break the work down when we get closer to delivery.

# 13 - Not clear on high level scope

Size of work items as we get closer to delivery

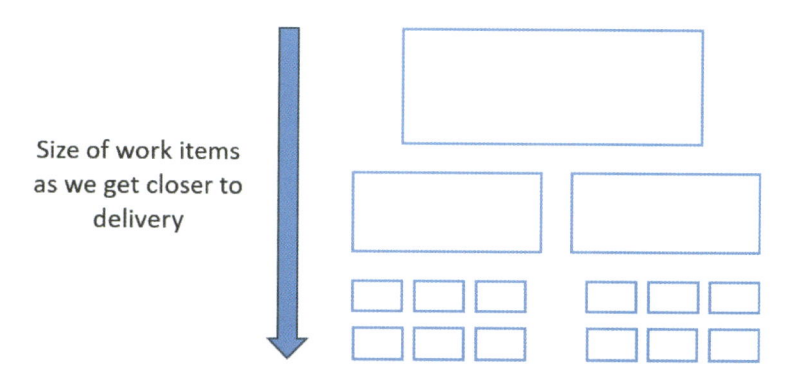

There are a number of benefits to this that we will look at below.

**Avoid work that doesn't get done**

If the feedback on the initial features takes us in a different direction we may need to change, delay, or throw away features we have already analysed. This is very wasteful particularly if the early feedback is that the product or features do not meet customer expectations and the whole idea should be stopped.

**Avoid delays between analysing and building**

If you have ever done part of a job then a while later come back to it you'll know that there's a cost to picking it back up again. For example, when I'm writing this book I've gone back to chapters that I've largely forgotten about and had to re-read them in full before making any further changes. This re-learning cost is particularly high for complex items. When doing all the analysis up front it could be months before you get to build and this re-learning is very costly.

## Requirements definition - User Stories

Here we will walk through a typical way of capturing requirements. User stories are captured in this format:

- As a [role]

- I want [a feature]
- So that [I can achieve a goal]

What this does for us is link the feature to a user need. Here is an example:

- As a trainee teacher
- I want an app to track my progress in the classroom
- So that I can ensure I successfully qualify as a teacher

So, we have a requirement written down, firstly this may be an assumption, we need to go and talk to the trainee teachers to confirm this is what they want. These highest level requirements are often called Epics. They follow the User Story format but it is clear they cannot be delivered without more detail and need breaking into more manageable pieces to understand them.

If this was written by someone that wasn't a trainee teacher you would have to confirm the overall assumption. The chapter on *Not structuring up front shaping* covers how to do this. Once we are clear this is worth building, we need to break the requirement down into manageable chucks. Below we have created two main features:

*Feature 1*

- As a trainee teacher
- I want to track my student's results
- So that I can see that my teaching is being effective

*Feature 2*

- As a trainee teacher
- I want to record any instances of bad student behaviour
- So that I can see if I am getting better with discipline

## User Story - acceptance criteria

To be even clearer we can use acceptance criteria. This allows us to **discuss** what we actually mean by these features:

As a trainee teacher
I want to track my student's results
So that I can see that my teaching is being effective

- Results of exams
- Feedback on high and low performers in regular lessons
- Results of homework

Now we have a lot more detail and a much better chance of building something valuable.

## User Story - additional artefacts

Even though acceptance criteria is helpful this should not replace additional useful artefacts. Don't make the mistake of thinking that User Stories now mean I don't have to do any further design work. We may have:

- A set of screen designs
- Some user journeys showing a typical scenario of a pupil behaving badly and how it is dealt with
- Some user personas to show me the types of trainee teachers and students I'm likely to be dealing with
- A technical design document that shows how the app will be built
- etc...

We can then put some of the customer focussed artefacts in front of the trainee teachers and get some feedback. We may find that they are very happy or having seen the concepts they don't think it'll work after all. This is all before building out a detailed user story backlog, and can save a lot of waste.

## 13 - Not clear on high level scope

**User Story - detailed backlog**

When I'm ready to build the first feature I can break this down further in order to deliver smaller parts. One simple way to do this is to take the high level acceptance criteria and split out the user stories from this.

As a trainee teacher
I want to track my students results
So that I can see that my teaching is being effective

- Results of exams
- Feedback on high and low performers in regular lessons
- Results of homework

Below you will see two examples of breaking down this user story:

**Example 1**
As a trainee teacher
I want to track my student's exam results
So that I can see that my teaching is impacting their grades

- For each exam I would like to:
- Be able to record the expected result of exam for each pupil
- Be able to record the actual result of exam for each pupil
- See where there is a big difference in expected versus actual

**Example 2**
As a trainee teacher
I want to track high and low performers in regular lessons
So that I can see if my style of teaching is working well

- At the end of each week I would like to:
- Record the highest performers
- Record the lowest performers
- Record those students who have performed much better or worse than expected

## Summary

Getting a handle on high level scope is really important for getting the right product and features out at the earliest opportunity. Start by being clear on your goals. Then define features to meet the definition of MMF or MBI. Finally, use techniques like User Stories and augment these will additional artefacts such as screen designs.

Progress tracking should include how many high level work items have been completed. Ensure that teams understand they should not spend a lot of time tweaking and changing features when there is low value in doing so.

It is also worth being clear to each team what the expected timelines are and that they should care about them.

# 14 - Not building in end-to-end slices

Here we look at the problem of teams building component parts of an end-to-end flow in isolation, then trying to put them together towards the end of the work.

- **The problem of** building in component parts rather than in end-to-end slices
- **affects** organisations that are scaling
- **the impact is** discovering late that systems don't work together, end-to-end flows fail testing, and expensive redesign and bug fixing is required

## Complex end-to-end flows

When building software, it is always best to keep things simple, by focussing on features that a single team can deliver on their own. When scaling to more than one team we can run into integration issues. Let's take a banking system, these are often very complex with many different systems talking with each other, along with complex business logic. There are teams dedicated to types of technology like a mainframe or specific business processes like reconciliation. Multiple teams are required, as the ability for one single team to effectively master both the business and technical knowledge isn't possible or practical. Due to this situation we end up with a variety of teams working on a complex end-to-end process:

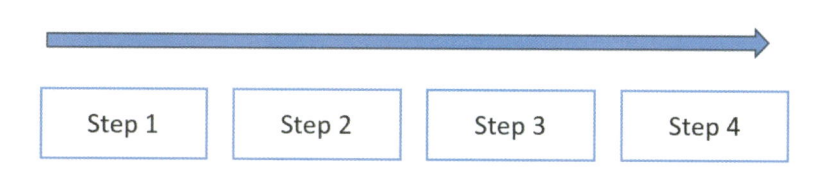

## Diving into the problem

The temptation within a large piece of work is for each team to focus too much on their own part of the process. Starting with a rough idea deciding what is required, then doing detailed analysis to build out their own work. Let's say you were Step 5 of a complex process, you have some understanding of what is being sent to you by the teams handling Step 4 and some understanding of what you are passing to the teams on Step 6. That can be best case! I have seen situations where the teams have no understanding of up and downstream work.

If you have dedicated integration test team you will find that they are usually first to surface the problem. They are running around trying to work out how to test end-to-end, but no-one can give them clear answers. This is an especially difficult task when they are not part of the requirements definition. Teams can push back against them being "annoying" when they try to take up time trying to pull everyone together. This cross team coordination can be seen as an interruption to valuable working time.

When teams are focussed on building their own component part you will find it can take a long time for enough functionality to be delivered to run even a few scenarios end-to-end. At this point virtually nothing works. The end-to-end test cases start failing at a rapid rate. There is then significant difficulty in knowing which team is responsible for the failure. The error appearing in a process at the end of the end-to-end flow doesn't mean it originated there.

Although the teams that are responsible for end-to-end testing may be reporting issues you can find that throughout the work each team was reporting "green" for delivery timelines, your healthy set up is now looking like a disaster.

I've seen this from a very experienced Agile consultancy who set up really impressive planning and monitoring set up but didn't have any control over the overall processes being built. This was mainly due to them having little expertise with business analysis. Early in the work it can seem like you are doing really well, but the iceberg is hidden under the surface.

## Seeing the big picture

To solve this problem, we have to start with a high level backlog of end-to-end flows. One way to do this is to visualise your user journeys. These are the path a customer takes when dealing with your organisation. This helps everyone understand the overall business model from a customer's perspective. You can see the steps the customer is going through, rather than starting on the back-end computer systems and how they interact. This allows business people to understand what is being built, where many software systems are interacting this can be obfuscated.

| User Activity 1 | User Activity 2 | User Activity 3 | User Activity 4 |

Building on the concept of user journeys are service blueprints, these expand to show how your organisation does its processing. Some of these activities are visible to the customer, for example when they need support, and others are not, for example an accounting team that is generating financial reports.

This view is very valuable for mapping existing pain points so that you can remove them. There are other business analysis diagrams that can help visualise flow such as UML Activity Diagrams. All these visual tools are extremely helpful when explaining complex systems. Service Designer and Business Analyst are the two common roles that would drive this type of work. On a large scale set up it is highly advisable to invest in these roles.

## Building in slices

Once we have understood the overall journey or high level process then begin to slice these up and deliver them end-to-end. It is advisable to work on simple journeys to start with. These are scenarios with no error conditions and simple logic. For example, you have an online shop, the customer chooses one item, enters all valid information and buys the product. You can expand on this after the simple end-to-end flow is working by adding logic like:

- What if they send the items to an address that isn't their home?
- How do I deal with delivering very large items?

Building like this does not mean we are going to release these flows to customers immediately, but we can start to test them. The overall look and feel can be reviewed by customers and our testers can check the basics work. Each system can be integrated early and checked for problems. It cannot be overstated how much risk is removed by these simple flows.

For very large systems there can be difficulty in creating large scale end-to-end software environments all in one go. In this case aim to test parts of the flow end-to-end, and prioritise environment creation.

## Planning the work

The goal in planning should be to bring the teams together to focus on delivering an end-to-end flow, not their component parts. They each work out what they need to build in order to make this work. This will lead to many conversations and you may need leadership to help facilitate these. In some cases, a dedicated analysis team is tasked with this. The success criteria should be made clear, it is not enough that your part of the process works in isolation.

## Analysis team anti-patterns

Although it is good to have individuals or a team that focus on delivering the overall end-to-end flows, they should not be working in isolation on the requirements. The expertise of individual teams should not be underestimated. If an analysis team works in a silo, you can find sub-optimal (or wrong) design late and it will be costly. You'll see this where teams tell you

- They simply can't plan their next set of work
- They have planned out the best they can be but it's probably wrong or it's very likely to change.

This team therefore focus on facilitating with the teams rather than doing all the work for them.

## Tracking the work

Shift from each individual team reporting "green" when having built their own component, to how many end-to-end flows are working. This also requires strong management oversight, usually from the leaders in business analysis and service design. If you can strengthen responsibilities for the success of end-to-end flows with specific people this will help.

It is **extremely** important if running timeboxed increments that you test end to end at the end of these. I have seen major failure from assuming the product is working based on teams delivering their own work on time.

## Summary

In scaled environments the delivery goal is relatively simple, it should be to incrementally produce working end-to-end flows. You should do all you can to get these into production like environments as soon as possible. Planning and progress tracking should take these flows into account to show the real health of your work.

# 15 - Not using live data early when replacing a system

Another factor that can cause major impact to your delivery timelines is not using live data early enough during development. This only applies to situations where you are replacing an old system and have existing data within it that requires migration.

- **The problem of** testing with live data late in the delivery cycle
- **affects** organisations that are scaling
- **the impact is** missing scenarios, broken processes, and late delivery

## Live data migration

This section covers considerations when working with live data.

### Poor quality live data

When developing new functionality, we are somewhat constrained by our old set up. In other words, we have to take into account data that has not gone cleanly through our new system. Let's use an example to demonstrate this. I allow only the values of 1 and 2 through a screen. Anything else is immediately rejected. The test team check this and it's working. The data that is migrated has the

15 - Not using live data early when replacing a system 95

value of 3 within it. This may have been from a previous bug or an old business process. The screen would have stopped the value of 3 going through but now it's there and it can cause unexpected errors in later processes.

We have some options here:

1. Cleanse the data that is being sent. We need to make a conscious decision with what to do with the value 3.
2. Handle the errors gracefully that are occurring due to value 3 being in the data
3. Do we make it into a 2? Do we add a new business model as it is a valid scenario?

## Database design

If we design a new database without considering the old database schema it can cause significant headaches when migrating. You should review the current design before making the new one.

## Migration planning and tracking

Consider having dedicated roles for migration and database design especially if the work is large and complex. These people become responsible for success. If possible, put them into the teams and if not have them join any planning events. It may also be beneficial to have a project manager planning and tracking progress.

## Data volumes

We can test our migration with smaller subsets of data. This ensures we don't put too much load on our live systems.

When ready we can also consider loading in all the live data to test with, as this can be beneficial for performance testing. We can now accurately simulate how our new system will cope with the current amount of data and it's complexity.

## Data backups

We need to ensure that data is recoverable at any stage.

## Data obfuscation

Some data may contain personal information and need to be obfuscated for use in test environments. There are tools that can help you with this.

## Incremental migration

I would strongly recommend migration as an ongoing activity rather than something to be done at the end. As features are developed complete the migration for them, this lowers the effort in the long run. Without this everything may look fine with simple scenarios being tested on clean data, then when the old data is ready defects occur everywhere. You don't have to migrate all the data. Some organisations will leave older data behind or choose not to migrate everything.

## Data security and compliance requirements

As you develop your new database ensure that these requirements are met. This may include:

- Data encryption
- Data encryption when in transit
- Data access controls
- Data protection for safeguarding specific sensitive information

## Production like environments

When designing our environments, we should look to make them as close to production as possible. In our new pre-production and production environments these may be full scale, in other test environments they may be less powerful but still be setup in the same way. Automated environment creation can ensure that environments are the same.

# Summary

Having a data migration strategy is very important. Run data migration alongside your delivery to reduce risk.

# 16 - Poor quality low level requirements

Having a good grasp on the higher level requirements is very important. We will now cover what happens if the lower-level requirements are not well done.

- **The problem of** poor quality low level requirements
- **Affects** organisations that are scaling
- **The impact is** unexpected team dependencies causing delay, bugs that are found late causing costly rework, scope getting unexpectedly larger
- **Affects** customers
- **The impact is** untested scenarios breaking for the customer leading to lower satisfaction

## Defining requirements

We covered some of the concepts such as User Stories and Acceptance Criteria in the chapter *Not clear on high level scope*. It is worth starting there before reading this chapter.

**User Stories and Acceptance Criteria**

Let's re-review the user story format as it's a very useful technique for defining requirements.

- As a [role]
- I want [a feature]
- So that [I can achieve a goal]

Using this example, we also see acceptance criteria that helps us understand the requirement in more detail. There should be a conversation after they are written.

As a trainee teacher
I want to track high and low performers in regular lessons
so that I can see if my style of teaching is working well

- At the end of each week I would like to:
- Record the highest performers
- Record the lowest performers
- Record those students who have performed much better or worse than expected

## The Three Amigos

To get a better perspective of our requirements we should invite multiple roles to review them. These roles can vary but bring different perspectives:

- Product owner - makes decisions on what should be built and guides the strategy
- Technical lead - has a view of the solution and its feasibility / cost
- Testing lead - a specialist in looking for different scenarios

Sometimes we add in a UX designer who may be checking the visual flow. This is a better technique than bringing in the whole team where some can be idle.

Let's simulate a conversation with the team being given this user story:

As a trainee teacher
I want to track high and low performers in regular lessons
so that I can see if my style of teaching is working well

## 16 - Poor quality low level requirements

- At the end of each week I would like to:
- Record the highest performers
- Record the lowest performers
- Record those students who have performed much better or worse than expected

The tester starts by asking what the highest and lowest performance means. In this case, they discover a quick test is run at the end of the week to see how well the lessons have been understood. The highest performers means those with the two top scores and the lowest are those with the two lowest. At this point, we change the acceptance criteria:

- Record the highest performers who are the two pupils with the highest scores
- Record the lowest performers who are the two pupils with the lowest scores

Some further questions are now asked, *"What does performed much better mean?"* This is when they have gone over 20% higher than their latest monthly average. Lower means 30% lower. The teacher would like to see the last month's average so they can calculate this manually. Again, updating the acceptance criteria:

- Record those students as "much better performance" where they have gone over 20% higher than their latest monthly average
- Record those students as "much worse performance" where they have gone over 20% lower than their latest monthly average

Now we get some more interesting scenarios, the tester asks *What happens if there is no recent average because someone has been away for a month or more?* The answer is to take the most recent available months score. If they have just joined the school then they don't go into the highest or lowest performance metrics until they've done at least a month. We can now add a new line of acceptance criteria for this. With unusual scenarios like this one, you can often find them breaking the software when it is in the customer's hands. These are the sort that teams can miss. When scenarios don't happen too often they can be difficult to debug and require the live data to analyse. This can be very time-consuming to fix.

Finally, the technical lead asks if all the results should be input in one go or one after another. This decision will affect the technical design.

It doesn't matter too much if you skimmed the detail above. The point being made here is the power of these **conversations**. We are looking to handle these scenarios gracefully, i.e. avoiding the software crashing. As unusual scenarios are discussed the chance of defects reduces.

### Behaviour-driven development

You may have noticed that capturing the scenarios from the conversation above could be tricky. Trying to think through all the things that could break. That's where behaviour-driven development, also known as BDD, comes in.

Looking at the acceptance criteria again and see how BDD would capture some of the previous conversations:

- At the end of each week I would like to:
- Record the highest performers who are the two pupils with the highest scores
- Record the lowest performers who are the two pupils with the lowest scores

Let's use a grid, which is an efficient way to display many scenarios. Within the grid, you will see examples of real data being used. Using real data is very powerful for team alignment and discovering unusual scenarios. This is a simplified example:

*BDD scenario - Recording weekly results*

| Pupil | Score out of 100 | Result |
|---|---|---|
| J Harris | 80 points | Highest performer |
| P Smith | 10 points | Lowest performer |
| M Webb | 42 points | Average performer |
| F Barnes | 60 points | Average performer |
| P King | 90 points | Highest performer |
| L Hubs | 9 points | Lowest performer |

When writing these scenarios you should aim to cover:

- **Happy path** where we have an entry that triggers no errors. These can be developed first to prove the software works.
- **Error conditions** where we deliberately try and break the software, for example by putting in a score of 101 out of 100, or a strange keyboard character in the pupil name field
- **Boundary conditions** for example if we put in the scores of 99 and 100.
- **Unusual scenarios** where the team deliberately try to break the process. In this case, we could have three people on 90 points, we now can't record the top 2 highest performers and need to decide how to deal with that.

BDD can also be performed using the sentence format of *Given, When, Then*. This was created by Daniel Terhorst-North. This business readable technique is often called the Gherkin syntax. There is a lot of information on the internet on this, so I will not deep dive into this here. To help you see how this works, I have shown how it would be written below:

*BDD scenario - Recording weekly results*

- **Feature**: Recording and analysing weekly test results

- **Scenario:** The two pupils with the highest scores are identified as "Highest performer"
- **Given** pupils have completed their weekly test with the following results

| Pupil | Score out of 100 |
|---|---|
| J Harris | 80 points |
| P Smith | 10 points |
| M Webb | 42 points |
| F Barnes | 60 points |
| P King | 90 points |
| L Hubs | 9 points |

- **When** the test results are analysed
- **Then** the highest performers are

| Pupil |
|---|
| J Harris |
| P King |

### User Interface prototyping

Visual prototypes can be very helpful to both development teams and customers. This is commonly known as concept testing. This allows you to check the flow and see if the overall business process makes sense. Imagine describing a house to someone versus sketching it, we can be very misaligned without realising it. With lower-level requirements, we are looking for more detailed screen flows, whereas at the high-level, it may just show a general design idea.

### Improving estimates

As we use these techniques to improve our understanding of our requirements, we can estimate better. There are different levels of user story maturity contained in the previous examples:

- User story on its own
- Unchecked acceptance criteria
- Acceptance criteria refined by the team
- BDD real data scenarios

We don't want to do all of our requirements up front to BDD standard however I would expect at a minimum for each user story to have acceptance criteria. It is a big anti-pattern not to have this. Imagine this previous user story, it would be completely impossible to estimate:

- As a trainee teacher
- I want to track high and low performers in regular lessons
- So that I can see if my style of teaching is working well

User stories can often hide really big pieces of functionality. With our acceptance criteria below, we discovered that there's complexity to how this should be delivered.

- Record those students who have performed much better or worse than expected

If originally the people estimating thought this was just a checkbox next to a student name, they may assume this was much smaller. To counter this it is recommended that a conversation is had, even if it's a quick one.

## Defining requirements at scale

Imagine your teams are dependent on each other and you only have a basic understanding of what is being built. This can lead to a user story being started then all of a sudden, another team is required. That team are now busy so the work gets parked. At some point, you need to pick it back up again and remember where you were. This can go out of control with a large number of teams dependent on each other causing major delays. It is really important to have a big-picture view of what you are doing first, then after this, you should work on refining the user stories together. Using UI prototypes and architectural diagrams can help a great deal with this.

The cost of a defect being found also becomes higher at scale, an unhandled scenario in a complex system can be difficult to track down. This requires multiple teams to take a look and track down the root cause. It can mean that defects are passed around the teams. By working on scenarios together you can avoid this.

## Summary

Don't underestimate the need for good quality requirements. Using techniques like user stories and BDD can help a great deal here. Combine these with visual artefacts like UI sketches to improve your understanding. At scale, this becomes particularly important as it helps you plan dependencies. Start with a good understanding of your high-level requirements, then get your teams to break these down into lower-level items as they go.

# 17 - Poor preparation for big room planning

One of the common methods for scaling is to use big room planning events. These are when all the delivery teams come together and firm up their backlog and dependencies, typically aiming to deliver over a time-boxed period. These time-boxes can be as long as 3 months. It is very powerful for building out lower-level requirements and aligning dependencies between teams. This can however be done very badly.

- **The problem of** poor quality preparation for big room planning
- **Affects** organisations that are scaling
- **The impact is** teams cannot plan well leading to scope creep and a wasted event

## Preparation quality

We covered requirements in the chapters *Not clear on high level scope* and *Poor quality low level requirements*. These chapters explain how requirements can be handled. We will now look at what should be done before big room planning events.

### High-level scope

High-level scope must be clear for the event. Having a good understanding of what needs to be built is the foundation for success.

In very large-scale development we may not be shipping after each timeboxed iteration. In this case building in end-to-end thin slices

## 17 - Poor preparation for big room planning

as defined in the chapter *Not building in end-to-end slices* is highly recommended. Early on in development, you are trying to reduce risk. Alongside slices, you may also be building out more complex areas to prove they work. This will give far more confidence to later estimates.

A good way to record the high-level scope is to use Epics. These are simply high-level user stories. By having a list of these you can track how many are being completed over time. The teams will also know what lower level scope should be created. A kick-off event led by a product owner and business analyst should be held to describe what is expected for the next timeboxed iteration. This allows the teams to go and work on their backlogs.

Typical symptoms of this being done badly are teams that are unable to plan anything. They may simply report that the scope is not clear yet.

**Entry criteria for planning**

One of the main mistakes I see teams making is bringing a very poor quality backlog of requirements to the planning event. This usually consists of poorly written user stories, sometimes just a title for them, and in many cases, this list is not complete. The teams then try to fix these during the event. This is very difficult especially if the timebox being used is a long one. What happens is instead of working with other teams to drive out dependencies they start to work through a few stories.

Typical symptoms of this are teams only a few weeks of items planned in and low confidence in their overall plan.

What should be done is the user stories and acceptance criteria should be defined before the planning event. The event is then used to plan dependencies with other teams and firm up the commitment. This requirements readiness requires work before the event. Each team should dedicate time to this. Stage gates before the planning event should be in place to check that:

- The high-level scope is clear (technical and business design)
- The team-level user story backlog is properly created
- User stories have at least some acceptance criteria
- An initial view of dependencies is clear

All of this should be done a few weeks before the planning event and teams that are not ready should be closely monitored.

In the planning event, the focus should be on firming up dependencies between the teams and commitment that the plan is achievable.

**Meeting in person**

There can be major benefits to teams meeting in person for these events. The ability to sketch on a whiteboard or huddle around a coffee. Although digital tools can be useful when there are a lot of people involved in meetings they can be difficult to manage. Face-to-face can also help to build friendly relationships especially when people have time to chat to each other about non-work topics. These stronger relationships help a great deal when there are difficult conversations about delivery later on.

## Summary

Don't underestimate the waste of time a planning event can be when high and low-level scope is not clear. These events should be used to firm up a plan with its associated dependencies.

# 18 - Suboptimal organisational design

Scrum creates an environment where a single team can control and optimise the process of delivering from an initial idea to working software in the hands of customers. There are often dependencies within a Scrum team, perhaps having roles for front-end and back-end engineers. These dependencies can be quickly resolved with face to face communication.

When scaling agile to more than one Scrum or delivery team we start to find difficulties. Face-to-face communication gets harder as more people are added, and we need to manage information passing carefully. As our delivery organisation gets larger, we are likely to see portfolio and programme management teams created to look at the big picture and provide strategic direction. This further complicates delivery efficiency as we see even more teams having to work together.

- **The problem of** inefficient team structures leads to additional complexity when working through dependencies
- **Affects** organisations that are scaling
- **The impact is** additional time lost to synchronisation and dependency planning leading to major delays

Organisational design is therefore a really important consideration when delivering at scale.

# Teams aligned to delivery stages

In some organisations you will find teams that are responsible for different stages of the delivery process. Value stream mapping is a Lean technique that helps us to expose how well these teams are working together. It maps out each process steps taken and the time each one takes including the delays between them. Here is an example:

| Product Team | Business Analyst | Scrum Team | Support Team |
|---|---|---|---|
| Create product idea | Create product backlog | Develop project | Deliver to live |
| 2 days | 6 mnths | 4 days | 3 mnths | 2 mnths | ½ day | ½ day |

Here we see a value stream map of the steps taken to deliver a project from idea to live. By creating this we give ourselves a window into how efficient a process is so we can improve it. Lean contains several principles and definitions of waste. We will reference some of these here to expose inefficiencies.

Creating a value stream map helps us to implement the Lean principle *optimise the whole*. We can now work out who is doing what process and be able to see how well different parts of the organisation are working with each other. In this example, we can see major delays between the stages. This is likely to cause two lean wastes, *hand-off* issues and *re-learning* as each team has to remember what they were doing several months ago during the handover.

Another waste classified by lean is *extra processes*, these may have been created to cope with inefficiencies caused by teams talking together. For example, the "create product backlog" step is being done by a business analysis team, this may be exceptionally detailed for handover to the Scrum teams. This separate process can be simplified or even considered for removal if the Scrum team could do it more efficiently themselves.

As we scale our delivery organisation and add more teams, the value stream map becomes an important tool that exposes how efficient our end-to-end delivery processes are. This tool allows us to assess the efficiency of our delivery, monitor delays and consider removing additional steps.

## Optimising teams

Before spending a lot of time fixing processes, you should review your organisational structure.

### Removing specialist teams

One solution to improving efficiency is to consider merging teams. You can avoid dependencies by being as **cross-functional as possible**. An external user acceptance test team is a good example of this. Moving these team members into delivery to focus on continuous user testing rather than a long end phase. This requires us to **think differently**, which can be difficult if you have hierarchical structures and career paths in place. The downside can be the size of the new team, this grows where there are too many specialisations. Therefore, we also need to consider cross-functional roles, for example, could the team's system testers take on system integration testing?

We can't always do this as we may have limited expertise in certain technology or business areas. You have some options here and you should consider these in the order listed below:

1. Are they a bottleneck and if so, is there enough work to justify upskilling more people?
2. Can we add specialist team members to the journey step aligned cross-functional teams (even if there aren't enough people to add one to each)?
3. If we can't remove the specialist team, are there other specialist teams they work frequently with that could be merged?

For example, you may have a front-end architecture team and back end architecture team. Make sure the teams don't get too big.

4. If we can't remove the specialist team can we improve the management of their work (improved planning and tracking)?

**Align Teams with Customer Steps**

In an ideal world, each team can work on any part of the software. You can simply funnel a piece of work into any team and it will be fully completed. There are major difficulties in achieving this in large and complex setups.

- Business knowledge becomes too big to understand the whole setup
- Technical knowledge of the codebase and sometimes differing programming languages

A way of splitting your teams up is to focus on specific customer steps. Let's take the steps of a training course:

| Register | Acceptance | Learn | Qualify |

For example, you may put a team onto the register stage. This allows teams to deliver entire steps. You can also put teams across multiple stages such as Register and Acceptance. You will still need coordination of your business strategy to ensure the entire customer journey works well. Standardising architecture and programming languages helps too, as it makes it easier to move people between teams with less effort.

# Organisation Restructuring Workshop

## Purpose

To improve organisational efficiency by optimising team structures. Please be aware that there will often be high levels of hostility to organisational change, therefore you may have to run this at the executive level and make difficult decisions.

### Process 1 - align teams to customer step

- Capture the high-level steps in your customer journey
- Map the ideal number of cross-functional teams to each step. Consider your strategic focus and your expected workload. For example, you may have a big focus on the qualify stage for the next year or the acceptance stage may always be small.
- You may already be able to map current teams to these steps. Don't spend too long on this as Process 3 may override your current team setup.
- Record any additional specialist teams that operate across the whole customer journey

### Process 2 - merge roles to increase efficiency

- For each role discuss
    - Could any roles be merged?

For example, could you merge a business analyst and a tester or a UX designer and researcher? Do not expect these to be easy conversations. In some cases, we are looking to improve the skill set of each role and not necessarily replace them wholesale. For example, we may want the UX designers to pick up some research work if there aren't enough UX researchers. Some may be easier

to merge than others, for example, a user acceptance tester and a system integration tester may be doing similar jobs.
- What upskilling would be required to succeed?

- You may still not be able to deliver the whole journey step if you have specialist teams and we should now evaluate these:
  - Are they a bottleneck and if so is there enough work to justify upskilling more people?
  - Can we add specialist team members to the journey step aligned cross-functional teams (even if there aren't enough people to add one to each)?
  - If we can't remove the specialist team, are there other specialist teams they work frequently with that could be merged? For example, you may have a front-end architecture team and back end architecture team. Make sure the teams don't get too big.
  - If we can't remove the specialist team, can we improve the management of their work (improved planning and tracking)?
- What processes will have to change to make this work? For example, a specialist test team may run a lot of testing at the end of a release, how could this be incorporated into the new setup?

**Process 3 - create ideal cross-functional teams**

- Map out what a cross-functional team structure would look like that could work standalone against each customer step. This would be a set of roles, they could consist of front-end developers, UX designers and so on.
- Assign people to the teams (if possible, keep the same teams and modify them)

**Process 3 - create a plan of action**

Including how you will:

- Communicate the change and its benefits
- Roll out the improvements to minimise delivery disruption
- Monitor the impact to delivery and morale, making changes as you gather feedback

## Summary

Changing your organisational design can be very hard, entrenched roles and processes can make any shift in working difficult. On the positive side, it can have significant benefits with reduced dependencies and more efficient working. Before you start to fix your processes review your structure.

# 19 - Too much work in progress

There can be a temptation for a senior team or product owner to keep adding scope to a delivery. As the delivery progresses new ideas emerge and missing functionality is discovered. This is very common when high-level scope is unclear as described in the chapter *Not clear on high level scope*. Delivery then starts to run late and the need to get through a backlog of work intensifies. Even if the team were previously working at a sustainable pace, the pressure builds. This can also lead to more and more items being pushed into the teams in the hope they will be done. Work in Progress is abbreviated to WIP.

- **The problem of** too much WIP
- **Affects** organisations that are scaling
- **The impact is** task switching leading to very poor delivery efficiency

## Lean and the cost of WIP

Lean is a term you often hear of in manufacturing. This is about maximising production by reducing waste. Its origins are from Toyota in Japan with its early implementation being called the Toyota Production System. Over the years Lean has been translated into software development helping us to understand how to work efficiently in an Agile environment. Below are the Lean principles. We will focus on *Eliminate Waste* when discussing high WIP.

- Eliminate Waste: Lean specifies 7 types of waste and focuses on removing inefficiencies
- Build Quality In: Practices that focus on quality to help remove waste at the source. In software development, this would be activities like TDD
- Create Knowledge: Building learning into our organisation. Including activities like teaching, working closely together and retrospectives
- Defer Commitment: By making decisions at the "last responsible moment" we avoid doing things before we have all the facts, which can lead to mistakes
- Deliver Fast: Get things to the market quickly to deliver value to the customer
- Respect People: Empowering people to make decisions, the exact opposite of command and control
- Optimise The Whole: Local optimisation can harm production. A simple example of this is where a team speeds up and starts passing more work to another team downstream, which creates a bottleneck. The two teams should have worked together on optimisation. Lean looks at the flow of work from idea to delivery and seeks to understand the effect of any changes across the board

There is a big focus on **working as efficiently as possible**. Note the principles of removing waste, delivering fast, and building quality in as big examples of this.

**Lean and WIP**

When we have too much WIP we end up not finishing our work items, simply task-switching between those in progress and grinding to a halt. In the book *Quality Software Management: Systems Thinking* by Gerald Weinberg, he provides an estimate of 20% additional cost for every additional project that a team member is working on. What this means is a huge cost when WIP increases. Let's consider why this cost occurs using me writing this book as an example. If I start work on a new chapter and then go back to an old one, I have to *relearn* where I was. When I switch back to the new chapter it's the same again. The cognitive complexity of the task exacerbates this cost. For example, if I'm writing a new chapter it will be much harder to get back into it compared to checking for spelling mistakes. Another example would be developers working on complex logic, the relearning cost can be very high. In some cases, a defect can take over a day to debug, and if continually interrupted take significantly longer.

There is also a concept of *flow state* developed by Mihaly Csikszentmihalyi. He describes this state as complete absorption in the current experience. This is an optimal state of engagement and therefore performance. It takes around 10 to 15 minutes to achieve this. Again, when task switching, there is a cost here. Therefore, the cost of task switching is not only when working on multiple items, but also when we are interrupted. Modern messaging tools can cause this to happen regularly. Teams should be made aware of these costs and adapt their behaviour, for example:

- Could recurring meetings be scheduled first thing in the morning?
- Can you delay any non-urgent messages until after 4pm?

All these smaller actions can add up to a great benefit.

## Delivering using Kanban

Kanban is a technique for controlling WIP. Kanban uses a board to track the work items in progress in their different stages, it also limits the work in progress in each stage to expose and tackle bottlenecks. Most people I have worked with do not know how Kanban boards work and are therefore not improving their flow of work. I typically show a board like the one below and ask, "Is this a Kanban board?".

19 - Too much work in progress                                    119

| Backlog | In analysis | In development | Live with customer |
|---------|-------------|----------------|--------------------|
|         |             |                |                    |

The correct answer is no. In this board when a work item is finished in the *In analysis* column it is **pushed** into the *In development* column. This creates a problem, if analysis is running faster than development many items can be pushed leading to high WIP. The items may not be being worked on as well. What we can visualise here is a bottleneck but we aren't solving it.

In a Kanban board like the one below you can see two columns for analysis and development. Now when an item moves out of the *In analysis* column it goes into *Analysed*. This represents work items that are not being actioned. This is pure **delay**. When we are ready, we **pull** the work item into *In development*. This shows us our true capacity.

| Backlog | In analysis | Analysed | In development | Development completed | Live with customer |
|---------|-------------|----------|----------------|-----------------------|--------------------|
|         |             |          |                |                       |                    |

The status of the work items is now accurate but we can still end up with high levels of WIP. The next step on the board is to limit the number of items in each column. This is called the WIP limit. Below we see the *In analysis* column with a limit of 4. This means that we should not put any more items into this column. In practice, it means a team will get stuck if there is a bottleneck as work items will pile up. With WIP limits we must **solve the bottleneck**, if you don't these boards aren't much better than any others! Another factor that can be considered is personal WIP limits. This stops people from having many items across multiple columns.

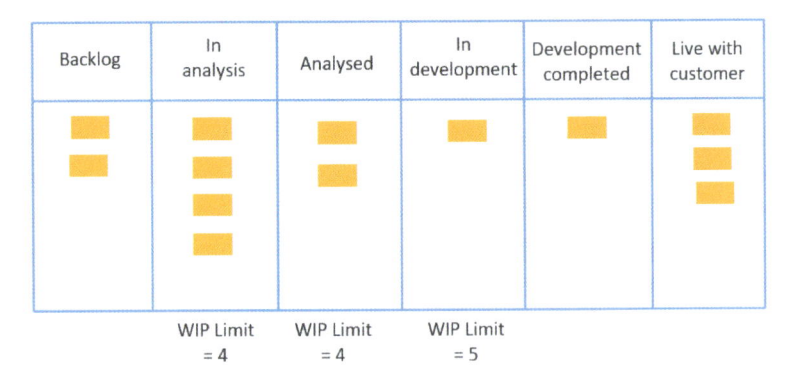

| Backlog | In analysis | Analysed | In development | Development completed | Live with customer |
|---|---|---|---|---|---|
|  | WIP Limit = 4 | WIP Limit = 4 | WIP Limit = 5 |  |  |

By following Kanban, we can get the value to market as fast and efficiently as possible.

## Summary

Kanban is an excellent method for visualising work, exposing bottlenecks, and reducing work in progress. This will lead to improved delivery efficiency. Remember you **must** stick to the WIP limits and solve the bottlenecks for this to work. Alongside this look to reduce day-to-day interruptions, as these can also slow your teams down.

# 20 - Lack of monitoring

Knowing where you are in a large-scale delivery should be a priority for any leader. One trap here is to rely on status updates from teams without tracking tools in place. You may get the feeling that things are going well and then get a shock when timescales get closer and the teams finally admit they are off target.

- **The problem of** a lack of progress tracking
- **Affects** organisations that are scaling
- **The impact is** unexpected late delivery

## Being re-active or pro-active

There is a lot of emphasis on retrospectives in the agile community. These focus on asking a team(s) to highlight issues that have occurred. Only using retrospectives can be very dangerous, as sometimes issues will build and build without us noticing, creating a critical failure when it could have been dealt with earlier. Consider poor unit test coverage, if we only notice after we start seeing very high levels of defects it then becomes very costly to build these back into our solution.

We need to be pro-active and build in real-time indicators to provide early signals when things are going wrong. This can act as an input to a retrospective. I would suggest you focus on three main areas:

- Progress - how are you progressing against your plan?
- Quality - as the Lean principle suggests do you "build quality in"?
- Flow - are you optimising how you work?

Let's take a look at how we could measure some of these. There are other measures, so please use this as a starting point.

## Progress indicators

Before we show how to do this let's cover an estimation technique. Story points are a unit of estimation for user stories. For example, I may have a user story that represents 13 points and another 5. These are **relative sizes** and don't reflect time. We can relative size between our user stories using this scale:

1, 2, 3, 5, 7, 13, 20, 100

The gaps between the numbers allow us to have a conversation about which user stories are larger or smaller than each other, and by how much. For example, a 2 is twice the size of a 1. As the items get larger this gets harder, so the gaps get bigger. We could be deciding if a story is either 7 or 13 points. This relative estimation is more effective than trying to estimate in time. Estimation in time is difficult, especially with large items where there can be large uncertainty and great inaccuracy. Below is a mapping technique that helps estimate a backlog of user stories.

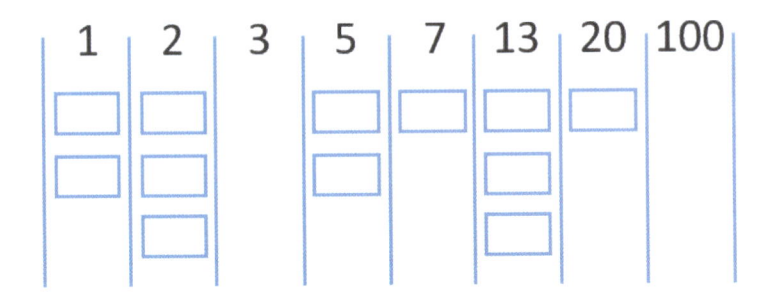

| 1 | 2 | 3 | 5 | 7 | 13 | 20 | 100 |
|---|---|---|---|---|----|----|-----|
| ☐ | ☐ |   | ☐ | ☐ | ☐  | ☐  |     |
| ☐ | ☐ |   | ☐ |   | ☐  |    |     |
|   | ☐ |   |   |   |    |    |     |

The technique shown is very useful, helping you ask if items are larger or smaller relative to **each other**. If you estimate stories on their own you may find people are secretly doing time estimates then assigning story points, which can be very inaccurate. To start your comparisons begin with a medium sized story and assign it 5 points. After this take the next story and ask if it is the same size, larger or smaller, and by how much.

Watch out for these estimation anti-patterns

- Conforming to the expert in the room. This typically means the detail behind the estimate is not questioned and even experts can miss things. Some expert developers are very fast and they may estimate low based on their own capability. This is terrible if that person is not in the team responsible for the work as it can cause the team to fail.
- Padding estimates
- Not learning from the accuracy of previous estimates. You should go back and learn where you went wrong.
- Inexperience leading to excessively high estimation. If you have inexperienced team members look to support them using techniques like pair programming rather than padding with high estimates.
- Not recognising when we don't know enough to estimate

The final anti-pattern is an important one. Large estimates for a single story such as 20 points, are a warning sign that either the item is too large and needs breaking down or it is poorly understood. When poorly understood we could do more analysis, however this isn't always possible or would take too long. Here are three additional techniques that can help. If you are doing multi-team planning you should do these activities **before** the planning event. This ensures that you understand your scope properly and can plan.

| Run a timeboxed spike | Build a prototype | Break into small tasks |
|---|---|---|
| Set a spike goal — Check results at the end — Set a number of days to achieve it | De-risk your implementation by building out a few user stories | |

## 20 - Lack of monitoring

These items are often picked up as feasibility risks when using the assumptions mapping technique. Assumptions mapping is covered in the chapter *Not structuring up front shaping*.

Now we are ready to plan out our work. When we deliver our user stories we can do this with a number of timeboxed iterations such as Sprints. In this case let's say each one lasts 2 weeks. We will see a total number of story points completed each iteration and this is known as velocity. Using an average velocity can help the team plan their future capacity. For example, if the average story point velocity is 20 every 2 weeks, I may plan to deliver my new stories as per the picture below.

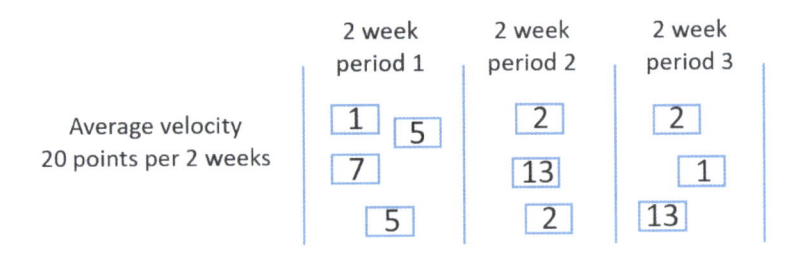

|  | 2 week period 1 | 2 week period 2 | 2 week period 3 |
|---|---|---|---|
| Average velocity 20 points per 2 weeks | 1  5 | 2 | 2 |
|  | 7 | 13 | 1 |
|  | 5 | 2 | 13 |

Notice that the team hasn't overcommitted here, it is better to pull work in from the next iteration if you finish early. If you are using Kanban and have no formal timeboxed iterations, you can still work out on average how many stories you deliver every 2 weeks (or whatever timeframe you choose) and plan accordingly.

In order to show overall progress against our plan, we have a few techniques you can use. Below is a product burn down that shows the progress over time. In this graph each sprint represents two weeks and we can see progress has slowed from sprint 3:

## Product Burndown

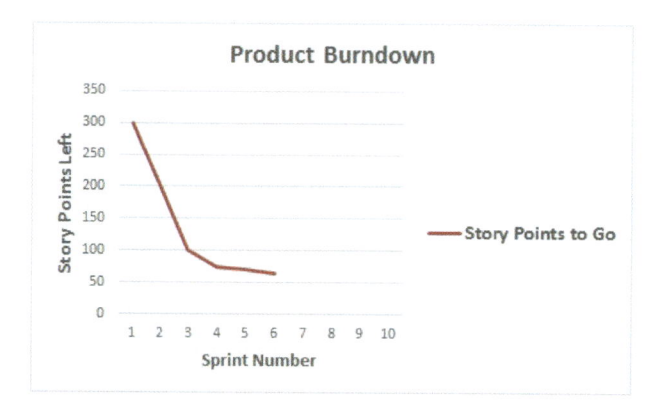

[Chart: Product Burndown showing Story Points Left (0–350) vs Sprint Number (1–10), with a line labeled "Story Points to Go" declining steeply from 300 to around 50.]

Another technique, which I prefer, is called the product burndown. This shows the relationship between scope and the team progress. The point where the dashed lines cross is a prediction of when the work is going to be complete. In this case it's around sprint 9. This product burndown shows a small amount of scope increase each sprint and a delivery speed of around 50 points per sprint.

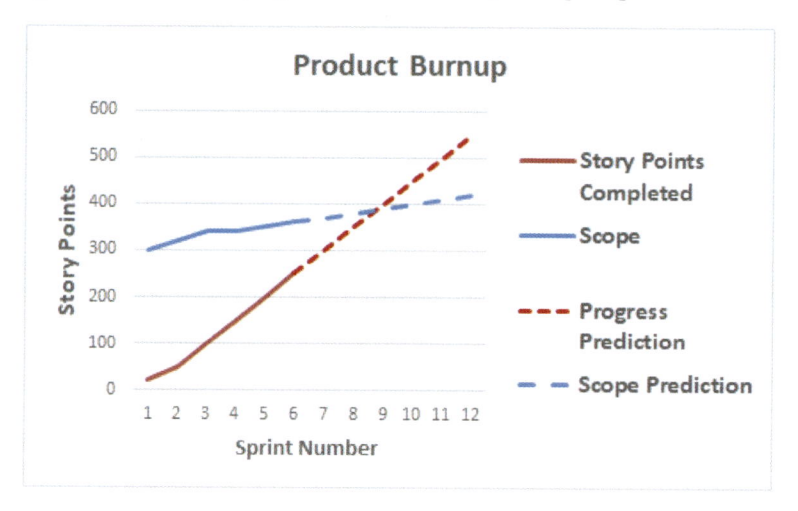

## Product Burnup

[Chart: Product Burnup showing Story Points (0–600) vs Sprint Number (1–12), with lines for Story Points Completed, Scope, Progress Prediction (dashed), and Scope Prediction (dashed).]

Having these two lines is very useful as you can see **why** we may be heading off target. In some cases, you can find scope out of control (like below) and in others the delivery speed may be slow.

**Product Burnup**

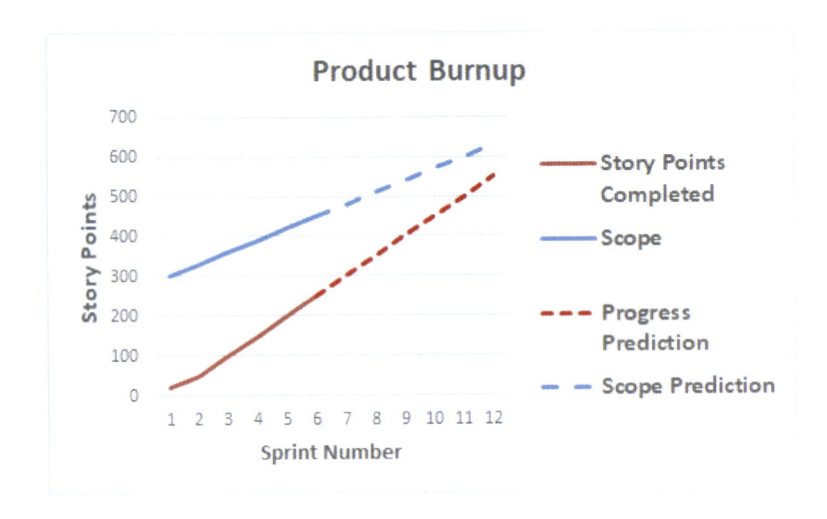

[Chart showing Story Points vs Sprint Number (1-12), with lines for Story Points Completed, Scope, Progress Prediction, and Scope Prediction]

## Quality indicators

*Unit test code coverage* - Unit tests check the lower level functionality is working and therefore you can use a lot of them.

*Number of defects* - To get the best value from this metric record the root cause. This helps you improve. For example, if it is down to poor requirements you can target this area to improve.

*Escaped defects* - The number of defects that escape into live.

*Static code quality* - There are tools on the market that can analyse your code base. Within this area are a number of measures such as cyclometric complexity that shows the complexity of a program.

*Dynamic code analysis* - These tools measure the code when it is running. This includes security, memory leaks, and runtime errors.

## Flow Indicators

Flow indicators can be done with Kanban boards as described in the chapter *Too much work in progress*. Having these in a digital format is recommended. Monitoring the flow of the high level and low level work items is recommended. This usually means you will have two levels of Kanban boards. The high level board tracks the high level requirements that may be shared across multiple teams. The low level board(s) are used at team level to track lower level requirements.

*Lead time* - This is the overall time a work item takes to progress through your Kanban board. A typical measure of this is from a customer request to the time it takes to deliver. This makes a lot of sense in manufacturing. In software development I often measure this from the time it leaves the backlog to live. Improving overall lead time is highly recommended. This is typically affected by the number of item in progress (WIP) and the size of items. Reducing both of these is highly recommended.

*Cycle time* - These measures represent the time it takes to pass through a particular delivery stage (or stages) within the lead time. For example, the time a work item takes in analysis. This is useful for looking for bottlenecks and optimising slow processes.

## Cause and effect

Let's say we've got a delivery with progress running slower than predicted:

**Product Burnup**

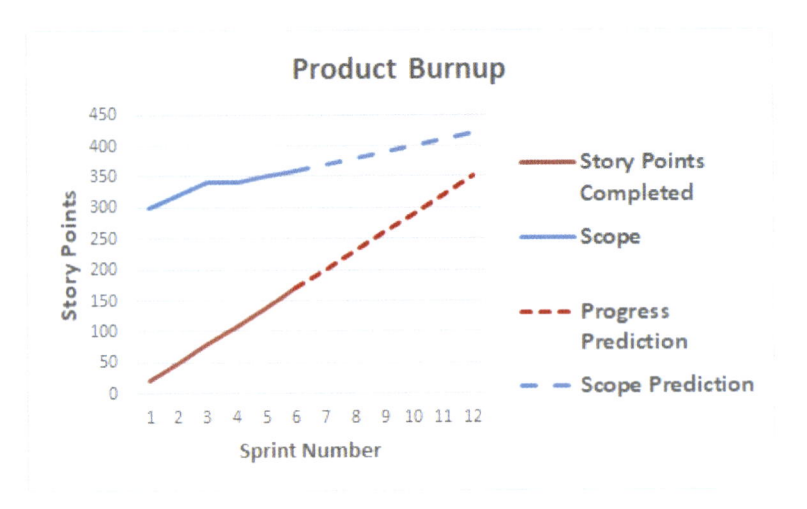

*Chart showing Story Points vs Sprint Number (1-12), with lines for Story Points Completed, Scope, Progress Prediction, and Scope Prediction.*

When making changes we rarely have a single cause and effect relationship. In other words what we tend to find is if we take action there can be expected changes, but also some that are completely unexpected.

### A typical response to a delivery running slowly

John the delivery manager has seen that progress is off target and delivery dates will be missed at the current speed. He discusses the lack of progress with his leadership team, and tells the development teams that they must work faster. This would seem sensible on face value, as he needs some urgency.

System's thinkers use diagrams to help understand these complex cause and effects loops. John is monitoring progress but not quality and flow. So let's look at what happens when John takes an action of pushing more requirements into the teams:

## 20 - Lack of monitoring

```
           Requirements
      S  ↙
              O
    Workload ←―――― Productivity
                                    O
  O
    Quality ――――→ Time spent on defects
              O
```

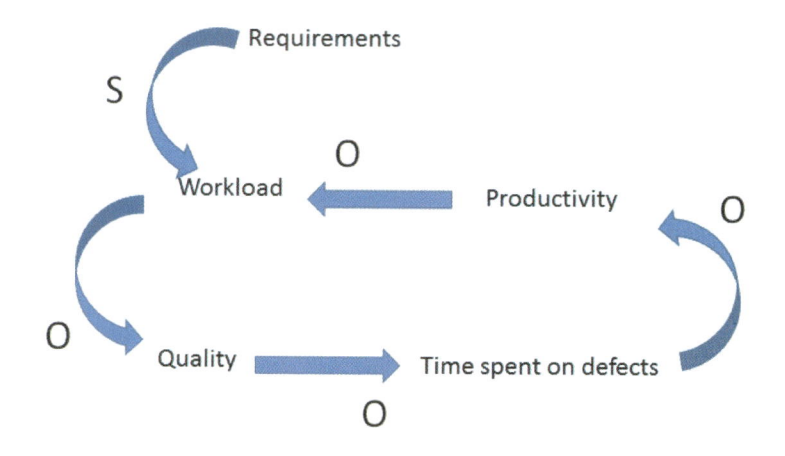

Impact of pushing more requirements:

1. To speed up, each product owner begins pushing more requirements into their team, and we see their workload increase. This is represented by an S on the diagram, which means there is a positive effect.
2. As the workload goes up the only way the team can sustain this is working long hours and over time the quality starts to go down. This is why we use an O on the diagram, it means there is an opposite effect. By pushing far more work on the team we see a negative trend occurring. This is a simple negative cause and effect. Systems that are in **balance** would be represented by a workload that ensures quality remains consistently high. It is important to understand that John believes that it is possible to keep the system in balance even with a higher workload.
3. Then what we see next is another adverse effect from quality going down, the time spent on defects goes up.
4. The time spent on defects then has a further negative effect on our productivity, again an O on the diagram, meaning it's the opposite effect.

5. Finally with productivity going down we see workload going up even more and everything grinds to a halt!

We've actually modelled what is known as a **vicious cycle**. We are spiralling out of control. This is the opposite of what John wanted. It can take a long time for John to see the workload dropping. The initial boost in productivity provided by working long hours is covering up the quality issues.

With retrospectives you may see some of these issues arising. However, retrospectives can be a slow feedback loop, issues are often prioritised only when things are badly broken. Another problem is the cumulative effect across all teams. If each team is only looking at their own data, they may consider the increase in defects as manageable, or accept the situation given the new pressure. When we add up the cost across all teams we see a very high cost. In summary, this means it is very risky to rely on retrospectives alone. We need to put in real time monitoring. By putting in quality indicators we see the number of defects rise by 20% over the month.

John may believe that his strategy works, he may firmly believe in it to the point of not being interested in others' opinions. *"We cannot miss this target, we must push the teams harder"* is a common conversation between managers responsible for deadlines and delivery teams that are off track. Hard data may be the only way to convince people who have firm beliefs that what they are doing is causing damage. Having this data early reduces the damage done.

This particular vicious cycle is why we see this agile principle:

- Agile processes promote sustainable development. The sponsors, developers, and users should be able to maintain a constant pace indefinitely.

This will not be what John wants to hear, he needs to make the deadlines. Estimation can be a root cause of timeline issues and it is important to assess this first:

1) The estimates were so far out that there is no chance of hitting the deadline with the current scope
2) The deadline was set with no estimation in mind and no matter what you do it won't fit. In these cases, there is no point pushing more work, you are just creating a death spiral

After this John should work with the teams on the levers to improve their speed, and ideally look to cut scope. There may be big problems with the way the teams are working together or the test strategy. Those people that are closest to the work can help a great deal with solutions but more so with identifying issues.

## Tracking trends

Let's use a scenario to explain why trends are important. A team measure their progress every sprint. They manage to complete 50 story points. They been praised by the leadership team as this is their highest ever result. The next sprint they achieve 30 points and a full review is conducted.

It is important not to overreact to individual results. This is simply natural variation. There may be many reasons for this variation, estimates may not be perfect, team members may be helping other teams etc. What is important is to consider the trend over time. If velocity is consistently increasing this should be celebrated.

## Summary

Create real-time indicators that track delivery progress, quality, and flow to get early visibility of issues. Ensure you consider trends and don't overreact to individual results. If things aren't going well, leverage the power of your teams for issue identification and solutions.

# Metrics Workshop

**Purpose**

To increase visibility into delivery progress, quality and flow

**Process**

Using the following categories to identify metrics. As a starting point you can also consider the metrics presented in this chapter.

- Progress - how are you progressing against your plan?
- Quality - as the Lean principle suggests do you "build quality in"?
- Flow - are you optimising how you work?

Consider identifying experienced people before you run this. If you don't have expertise you may need to do some further studying before you start. For example, in flow you should understand lead and cycle time.

1. For each category

- What should we track?
- Where can we get this data?
- If it is not available now, how could we get it? Note: a good metric should be easy to capture, those that take a lot of effort are not recommended.
- Can we automate the gathering of the data?

2. Who will track this data and implement improvements?
3. What governance is required?

**Output**

- A set of indicators
- A set of owners
- A governance structure

# 21 - Lack of project management skills

The importance of planning, dependency management, managing risks and issues and tracking progress should not be underestimated. My personal experience is that almost all delivery leads will tell you that they are good at these aspects, however I find many are not. It requires good governance and attention to detail to expose these weaknesses early. Teams working at scale that do this poorly can cause a scaled set up to fail.

- **The problem of** a lack of project management skills
- **Affects** organisations that are scaling
- **The impact is** poorly co-ordinated teams and late delivery

## Multiteam planning

The idea that Agile means no planning is a myth, the Agile Value is actually:

- Responding to change over following a plan

As per the word "over", this means that change is prioritised and not that planning is ignored. When working with multiple teams there is a need to plan and co-ordinate dependencies. If one team is supposed to deliver a piece of work that another team is dependent upon within a specified timeframe and doesn't, there will be blockages. If there are multiple teams and dependencies the whole delivery can grind to a halt.

Planning is often underestimated as a skill and it can be assumed that anyone can do it. I personally believe this is not the case and the project management skillset is underrated. You will often see teams that are working within timeboxes without this skill having a poor grasp of their progress against a timeline and delivering late.

### Planning and tracking techniques

In the chapter *Lack of monitoring*, in the *Progress indicators* section, I cover planning and tracking techniques using story points in detail.

### Dependency management

If we are using timeboxed iterations like Sprints we can plan out dependencies using them. This can also be done in a traditional project plan by tracking specific delivery dates. If you are multi-team planning this is a key artefact. Dependencies should be closely tracked as these can de-rail delivery dates if not managed well. The picture below shows how a team can record these.

Team D

| Dependent on team | Expecting work / giving work to | Sprint 1 | By when | Sprint 2 | By when | Sprint 3 | By when |
|---|---|---|---|---|---|---|---|
| Team Y | Giving work to | User story 133 | End of sprint | | | | |
| Team Z | Expecting work | User story 155 | 03/04 | | | User story 188 | Start of sprint |

# Risk and issue management

Another simple question to ask your delivery leads is the difference between risks and issues. For reference, a risk is something that **could** happen, and an issue is something that **has** happened. Below is a simple explanation. You should look to implement a formal risk and issues management process with governance.

Managing risk means

- Clear risk ownership

## 21 - Lack of project management skills

- Formulating mitigation strategies to avoid them
- Actively managing the mitigation to stop the risk becoming an issue

Here is an example risk log with its associated scoring matrix. Note the word *probability*, which means it hasn't happened yet. We can also choose to accept the risk. This is common when the mitigation is very expensive. Avoid raising risks with low probability and impact unless you have a very good justification. We need to be very careful if brainstorming risks. If you do this you will often see the anti-pattern of many low probability / high impact ones being raised. For example, *there will be another global pandemic derailing our delivery timeline.* This is very unlikely to happen given the timeframe and it is not worth attempting to mitigate against.

Risk log

| Risk Date | Risk Description | Risk Probability | Risk Impact | Risk Score | Mitigation Strategy | Risk Owner | Risk Status Not started, In Progress, Risk Mitigated, Risk Accepted |
|---|---|---|---|---|---|---|---|
| 01/03 | There is a risk that User story 133 will not be delivered in time | 2 | 3 | 6 | Stop work on user story 122 | Jake H | In progress |

|  | | | | | |
|---|---|---|---|---|---|
| | Very High (4) | 4 | 8 | 12 | 16 |
| | High (3) | 3 | 6 | 9 | 12 |
| Probability | Medium (2) | 2 | 4 | 6 | 8 |
| | Low (1) | 1 | 2 | 3 | 4 |
| | | Low (1) | Medium (2) | High (3) | Very High (4) |

Impact

Managing issues means

- Clear issue ownership
- Formulating plans to solve the issue
- Actively managing that plan

Here is an example issue log with its associated scoring matrix. Issue urgency can change over time. Let's say we haven't performed security testing by the middle of the delivery, this may become very urgent and need immediate attention as we approach the release date.

Issue log

| Issue Date | Issue Description (ideally quantified) | Issue Urgency | Issue Impact | Issue Score | Actions to Resolve | Issue Owner | Issue Status |
|---|---|---|---|---|---|---|---|
| 01/03 | Architecture for database is unclear 3 teams are delayed by 2 weeks | 4 | 3 | 12 | Architecture board in emergency session to resolve | Sophie H | Not started |

|  |  | Low (1) | Medium (2) | High (3) | Very High (4) |
|---|---|---|---|---|---|
| Urgency | Immediate (4) | 4 | 8 | 12 | 16 |
|  | High (3) | 3 | 6 | 9 | 12 |
|  | Medium (2) | 2 | 4 | 6 | 8 |
|  | Low (1) | 1 | 2 | 3 | 4 |

Impact

With lower maturity you may see organisations that record items but don't manage them well. It is important to regularly look for new risks and issues too, this is not a one off exercise. If you are doing big room planning, formally record risks and issues during the event.

## Summary

You should regularly assess your project management maturity

- Do your teams plan well and closely track progress?
- Are dependencies formally managed as part of planning?
- Do your teams often run late?
- Was the risk of running late raised early?

- Are risks and issues regularly considered, raised and actively managed?
- Is scope added without any impact assessment on timescales?

These important skills will help you delivery more successfully.

# 22 - Suppliers competing

When you have multiple suppliers on a scaled project there are risks involved. This is not always a problem but it is worth being aware of.

- **The problem of** suppliers competing
- **Affects** organisations that are scaling
- **The impact is** poorly co-ordinated teams and late delivery

## Supplier dynamics

A supplier will have a commercial interest in maintaining and often growing client accounts. In a perfect world all suppliers would not be competing and trying to help a client as much as they could. This is not always the case when there is competition involved, and although it may not result in conflict it could manifest itself in a lack of cooperation.

If you are in a situation where you may have competing suppliers carefully manage the following:

- Are the teams working well together?
- Is there any conflict arising around ways of working or direction?

Seek insights from the team members on the ground. Don't rely solely on the senior team for information.

## Sole supplier

Although you could view having multiple suppliers as "*spreading the risk*", by being able to replace those who are not doing well, you may be adding risk. You are actually spreading delivery accountability. This can result in finger pointing when things go wrong. Having a sole supplier can be beneficial here as they will have more incentive to step in and fix a delivery that isn't going well. If you have multiple suppliers you are also working with multiple management teams, this can add further complexity.

## Structuring multiple supplier set ups

One option is to create different delivery teams per supplier. The idea here is that they are accountable for their own work. The downside is they may not coordinate well with other teams. I have seen this at the extreme where two different suppliers created two different databases for the same thing! They were working entirely in silos for months.

Another option is to mix team members together, for example, one supplier may provide the UX design people. The downside being accountability for delivery is now diluted.

## Strong oversight

I would strongly recommend the following:

1. Having delivery roles filled by your own people, so that they are close to the detail. For example you may have a Scrum Master at a team level. This provides low level insight and can help with interpersonal relationships.

2. You should have suitably senior people overseeing areas such as testing. Senior does not just mean a leadership ability, but also a strong skillset. You may bring contractors in if you don't have these people in house. If you have strong trust in a person that works for a supplier this may be OK, but adds some risk as they may have divided loyalties.

## Regular retrospectives

By running regular retrospectives you can surface issues. This isn't perfect as some people may be guarded with what they say. It can also foster improved collaboration when multiple suppliers are working on solutions together.

## Summary

Be aware of multi-supplier dynamics and stay close to potential conflict that leads to inefficiency. Try to reduce the amount of commercial competition where possible. Consider a one supplier set up and embed your own people into key positions.

# 23 - Inexperienced leadership

It is all very well to have the most comprehensive and suitable scaled framework, but a lack of skill can derail success.

- **The problem of** poorly skilled leadership
- **Affects** organisations that are scaling
- **The impact is** unforeseen issues arising and late delivery

## Leadership experience

Using myself as an example, when I set up my first scaled project I encountered a number of the issues in this book. However, I didn't know they were a problem until later on when delivery started to run late. There is a temptation to rely on our experience in previous jobs, where we have been successful, and expect to see this success continue with new techniques. Experience is vital to success. I was given a very junior team as well, with inexperienced people running testing, and leading the teams. This simply compounded this issue and caused confusion. In some cases, I did know how to fix things but didn't have the time to do it, as the knowledge gap was too large.

## The training trap

There is an assumption that if you put everyone through training courses they will gain enough skills to be successful. If this were true we could simply run sufficient training for any profession and then put that person straight into a senior position.

Tacit knowledge is a useful concept here. This is the knowledge that people have that they cannot express easily. Let's take OKRs as an example, I teach and mentor people on these regularly. Even though to me they seem relatively straight forward this is due to having extensive experience. Some of the people I work with still struggle with them even a number of months later. This tacit knowledge is a hidden skill, and because it is hidden you can fall into the trap of believing that training people or giving them an answer, means they can do a job as well as you. You have underestimated your own skill.

The writer Malcolm Gladwell wrote that mastery is based on practice. When learning musical instruments it would take around 10,000 hours to become a master. To me, the exact timescale applied here doesn't matter, but the concept is important. I don't think it takes that long to get good at OKRs, but it may take that long to lead in a profession. You should treat training as the foundation from which you can begin to practice.

## Supporting people through change

Leading on from training we should ensure we are providing adequate support to the leadership and teams to help them be successful. Using expert coaches or consultancies can help here. Be careful that they are not doing all of the work, this means you won't be improving.

Why are coaches useful? It is simply that they have the time to help people improve. Being focussed on helping people and not trying to do another role at the same time, means you are more likely to see success. I have been in senior delivery roles where I simply didn't have the time to help people properly. This is not only frustrating, but very painful, when you see things failing around you that you could have fixed.

Applying this back to the 10,000 hours figure, if the team are practicing OKRs they need to know if they are getting these wrong. I could do 10,000 hours of the wrong thing and I've mastered nothing! The quality of practice is important and this is what a coach can provide. The feedback from an expert helps the person learn properly. You'll also find that people learn at different rates and a skilled coach can help by assigning their time effectively.

## Creating the wrong set up

A major problem with having inexperienced leadership is that they can create the wrong delivery set up and not realise it. Perhaps you have a process where everyone is working in silos, or not tracking the high level scope. The teams may be happy with this, especially at the start of the work. Success is seen as performing the first few planning events or seeing some software being produced. It is only later on that you realise that the scope is out of control and the teams' software doesn't work together. At this point it can be very difficult to perform a reset, processes have become embedded and teams comfortable in what they are doing.

Another problem here is the previous investment in improving the existing broken process. Teams may have got better at how they plan and be very happy with that, but then they are disrupted by being given a new planning technique.

## Recruiting carefully

When you are recruiting for a senior position make sure you have sufficient skills to do this properly. If I were to interview a number of chefs I would have some idea of what they do, but would not be qualified to judge them. Bringing in the wrong person can be very expensive. It is also easy to be wowed by their skills, as they will be talking about a lot of things you don't know much about.

## Summary

Focus on creating a properly skilled leadership team to ensure you succeed. If you do this right you will get good processes and practices in early. Use coaches and consultancies who have the time and space to help people as you deliver.

# 24 - Transformation without business involvement

If your scaled Agile transformation is being led by engineering and delivery leadership you can end up missing out on the business benefits. In many organisations, the business leadership and technology leadership are split. Delivery can end up focussing on planning efficiency and not improving what is built. What is needed here is an equal focus on business agility, which in simple terms, as defined as the ability to quickly respond to market changes and customer demands.

- **The problem of** transformation without business involvement
- **Affects** organisations that are scaling
- **The impact is** a focus on delivery efficiency above that of business agility

## Lack of business involvement

This is a common anti-pattern found when a transformation consultancy is composed of Agile coaches with a predominantly delivery background. These people will have become experts at planning and multi-team coordination. They will then focus on this team coordination and progress tracking. This all looks good, but the business are being left behind. In my experience, it is unusual to find Agile coaches with strong product experience. Where they do tend to have skills is in their knowledge of user stories and techniques like BDD. However, the ability to understand how to transform the way a business strategy is defined is a step beyond their abilities.

Another problem even skilled coaches will have is being given an open door to review how strategy is done. Organisations can push back against this, allowing coaches to work with team level product owners but not focus on the strategic processes that need transformation.

## Business transformation

If you are working in a scaled environment or are about to undertake the deployment of a new process, ensure that the business people are part of the leadership team. The business should have an understanding of their transformation journey too. For example, you may be moving away from a fixed one (or more) year plan to a Kanban based backlog that changes based on results. You may want to drop projects entirely and focus on the continuous flow of work into permanent teams. Your strategic inputs from customers could be strengthened, by conducting regular research and implementing techniques like customer journey mapping. You may shift from a 1-year strategic cadence to 6 months and have more regular results meetings.

## Bringing in the rest of the organisation

As you start to deliver faster you will find that the rest of your organisation needs to keep pace. It is not good enough to simply ship new features to customers if they cannot be supported or have not been marketed properly. You may also find you now have a sales team that is not skilled in your latest product.

This means your cross-functional teams need to expand, they should not just consist of developers and testers, they now need to consider marketing and the wider interfaces into the business. Now this doesn't mean you need a new marketing person in every team, but they must keep up with the cadence of delivery. In some cases, they may ask you to bundle up multiple features for a better Go to Market (GTM) strategy.

## Summary

Do not underestimate the challenges of transforming a business to one that is truly practicing the Agile values and principles. Make sure the business people are major players in any transformation and focus on creating an organisation with improved business agility. Look for partners with business transformation experience to help you with this.

# Conclusion

Whatever way of delivering at scale you choose, you will likely encounter one of more of the problems described in this book. In some cases the chapters are introductions to very large subjects (such as BDD) and it will be beneficial to seek out experts to help you further. I hope you have found this material helpful.

Thanks for reading! Timothy.

# References and book copyright

The following chapter covers

- the book's copyright
- references to external work that has been used

## Copyright for this book

This work is licensed under a Creative Commons Attribution-NonCommercial-NoDerivatives 4.0 International License. For full details see this link (correct as of 18/03/2024) https://creativecommons.org/licenses/by-nc-nd/4.0/

## References

All website links are correct as at 1st February 2024. These may change over time.

### Chapters 1, 3, 4, 5 & 6
Agile manifesto copyright 2001 (the 17 authors on the following site)
https://agilemanifesto.org/
*Usage in the book* - Values and principles from the manifesto are quoted.

### Chapters 1
Nexus Framework is Copyright © 2024 Agilest LLC. AGILEST®

*Usage in the book* - Nexus Framework is only mentioned and none of their material has been used.

### Chapters 1 & 3
SAFe®, Scaled Agile Framework® is copyright of © Scaled Agile, Inc.
http://scaledagileframework.com
*Usage in the book* - SAFe is only mentioned and none of their material has been used.

### Chapter 9
*Cynefin Framework as at February 2021 by Dave Snowden – thecynefin.co*
The Cynefin Framework as of February 2021 - reproduced under Creative Commons Attribution 4.0 International licence from Cynefin.io (2021). Cynefin is a registered trademark.
*Usage in the book* - The official version of the Cynefin Framework is used.

### Chapter 5
Competing Values Framework (CVF) - Quinn R. E., Rohrbaugh J. (1983). A spatial model of effectiveness criteria: Towards a competing values approach to organizational analysis. Management Science, 29, 363-377
*Usage in the book* - The CVF is reproduced.

### Chapter 6
Teaching Smart People How to Learn (Harvard Business Review, May/June 1991), Harvard Business School professor Chris Argyris
*Usage in the book* - the findings of Chris are used with no direct quotes.

### Chapter 16
Daniel North - Introducing BDD
https://dannorth.net/introducing-bdd/
This introduces the Given, When, Then syntax. This is commonly done in a business readable format called Gherkin.
*Usage in the book* - My own example of Given, When, Then is used

# References and book copyright

in the book. No other material is used.

## Chapters 1 & 3
PRINCE2 Agile and PRINCE2 are registered trade marks of AXELOS Limited
https://www.axelos.com/
*Usage in the book* - Principles from PRINCE2 are quoted.

## Chapter 6
HSE Guidance - Human factors: Fatigue
https://www.hse.gov.uk/guidance/index.htm
*Usage in the book* - A principle from the guidance is quoted.

## Chapter 19
Quality Software Management: Systems Thinking by Gerald Weinberg
*Usage in the book* - Findings from Gerald are used with no direct quotes.

## Chapter 23
Malcolm Gladwell - Outliers: The Story of Success
*Usage in the book* - Findings from Malcolm are used with no direct quotes.

Printed in Great Britain
by Amazon

3d61af7e-80b8-4479-be02-ee70ac3affb3R01